PRAISE FOR THE BOOKS BY TG WOLFF

"TG Wolff's Detective De La Cruz is caught in the crosshairs of solving heinous crimes, defending himself against a wrongful lawsuit, helping an abusive drug dealer's family, thwarting his mother's matchmaking, and falling in love. Pit against those who subvert justice and twist the law to suit their own ends, Cruz stands true while suffering his own demons—everything a hero should be. Wolff's unsentimental and precise writing draws readers. Add *Exacting Justice* to your 'to be read' pile."

—E. B. Davis, mystery author

"Working with an incarcerated population, I deal regularly with people who have made poor life decisions but who can be inherently funny, surprisingly talented, or overly concerned. I know that simple labels of 'good' and 'bad' don't work in the real world. In *Exacting Justice*, TG Wolff created characters just as messy, complicated, and dynamic as real life that keep you wanting to read page after page."

—Vincent Giammarco, Director of Behavioral Health Care

"TG Wolff's novel is for crime-fiction fans who like it action-packed and hard-edged. Written with feisty panache, it introduces Diamond, one of the most aggressive, ill-tempered, and wholly irresistible heroines to ever swagger across the page."

—David Housewright, Edgar Award-winning author of *Dead Man's Mistress*, for *Widow's Run*

SUICIDE SQUEEZE

BOOKS BY TG WOLFF

The De La Cruz Case Files
Exacting Justice
Driving Reign

The Diamond Mysteries
Widow's Run
Suicide Squeeze

TG WOLFF

SUICIDE SQUEEZE

DOWN & OUT BOOKS

Down & Out Books
3959 Van Dyke Road, Suite 265
Lutz, FL 33558
DownAndOutBooks.com

Cover photograph by Eneida Nieves
Cover design by JT Lindroos

ISBN: 1-64396-177-2
ISBN-13: 978-1-64396-177-4

For my father-in-law, Mort.
Here's hoping this one is better
than choking down a blueberry blintz.

MUCH TO DO ABOUT NOTHING

Today was a good day to die. I should know—I picked it. Of all the days in all the years, this was the one when everything would come full circle and I would see my husband again.

If you believe in that sort of thing.

Which it turns out...I do.

My name is Diamond, and I'm a list maker. If it makes me a nerd, well, it's not the worst I've been called. For all you list makers out there, I did the impossible. I finished my list.

Sound like I'm bragging? I'm not.

Do you know what a list maker does when the list is finished?

Nothing. Absolutely nothing.

There was no point to me anymore.

There were no details left to do. The house was clean, garbage taken out. My accounts were settled, and the letter turning over my shell company was easy to find. Donations were made of everything extra I had. I was done.

In my bedroom, I sat on my bed and took off my boots. Spring was edging toward summer in this not-so-trendy part of Washington D.C., but the hardwood floors were cold on my feet. My wedding picture sat on my nightstand. The silver-plated frame was a wedding gift. I don't remember from whom. The face I loved to wake up to smiled out at me. I touched his cheek, remembering how his whiskers scratched, missing the way he buried his face into my neck just to make me squeal.

I picked up my gun.

The three of us went into the bathroom and climbed into the tub.

This time, death would be simple. It was just me and a bullet. Diamond and lead.

The man who would find me, Ian Black, knew how to take care of a body. The plot where my husband was buried had a "hers" side. There was a coffin in it and a body that wasn't mine. A necessary part of burying my past life. Now, I wished I had figured out a way to get into my coffin. I wanted to be buried next to Gavriil Rubchinsky. I knew it didn't matter where my body was. Six feet deep, bottom of the river, burned to ash, it was all the same. I was going to meet him where bodies didn't matter.

Still, it would have been nice.

A bullet for my heart. Broken as it was, it would still bleed. Hence the tub and my uncomfortable position over the drain. The classic is the headshot, which is fine if you don't give a shit about whoever is going to be cleaning the mess. I had a seventeen-year-old kid squatting across the hall. Andrew Dixon. I didn't want him to see me like that.

I touched my husband's face, feeling his warmth instead of the cold glass. "I hope you put a good word in for me." My voice broke. "I'll need—"

The back-gate buzzer sounded like a National Weather Service warning. I jumped, smacking my head on the spigot. Fuckin' A, that hurt. The buzzer sounded again, and I fumbled Gavriil's picture. He fell out of the tub and landed with a smash on the white hexagon tiles.

"What kind of world is this coming to when a person can't get fifteen minutes of peace and quiet!" I climbed out of the bathtub and shoved the narrow window as high as it would go. "What! What could possibly be important enough to lay on that buzzer like a whore on a broken mattress?"

"I? What? I'm not a whore!" The blonde outside my gate clucked like a hen, then pushed the damn button again.

"Bitch!" I elbowed the screen until it popped out, then shoved my gun hand out. "Do it again. I dare you." The screen hit the pavement with a crash. Her hand reached for the damn buzzer. "What do you want?"

"I'm looking for Diamond. Please tell me you're not her." My Interruption wore designer black pants and an elegant white shirt. Her hair was wild in the breeze, her face one I'd never seen before.

"In the flesh. Doesn't tell me what you want."

"I have a problem." Her gaze swept around the parking lot.

"Welcome to the club. Try Jack on the rocks." I started to pull back.

"I got a note," she said hastily.

"Good for you. I'm sure your mommy's proud."

"He...he said you had to read it."

This was getting old. "Who?"

"His name is O'Rourke." Her voice drifted. "He wants to help."

"Then go lay on his doorbell."

There was bite in her voice this time. "He told me *you* could help me."

"He was wrong," I said, showing teeth of my own. She tore open the letter. "Did you say that was addressed to me? You can't open it. It's against federal law!"

"Arrest me." She held the paper between both hands, her brows tightening. "This doesn't make sense."

Don't ask.

Don't ask.

"What the fuck does it say?"

"It's an IOU from you to someone named Sam Irish. Good for, and I quote, 'One favor you can call in anytime, except the hours of two a.m. to four a.m., anyplace, except Malta, the Yucatan Peninsula, and Gary, Indiana, for any reason, unless it's stupid.'" She looked up at me. "It's only seven, we're in Washington, D.C., and it's not stupid."

"Ha! Of course it is." I waved the gun triumphantly, catching her in an ipso facto. "It's all stupid!"

"My husband's been kidnapped," she shouted, her voice breaking on the last word. "He's been missing for two days. The police don't believe me. They think he's run off with a mistress."

I froze, my arm, head, and shoulder out the window. "Fucking Irish," I muttered, looking to the sky. A crow circled overhead, swooping lower on each turn. "We're not going to let him mess this up, are we?" A maniac robin appeared out of nowhere. The streak of orange raced between the buildings, banked right, hung left, and crapped on my gun hand. "Fucking karma."

"I'm not crazy, but I am desperate. He didn't leave me. I know he didn't. He...he wasn't that kind of man." Her mouth kept moving, her words turning to *blah blah blah* as my gaze drifted to my husband's face smiling out through shattered glass.

When the shaky video surfaced, showing Gavriil stumbling into the street, everyone I went to—the Italian police, the American consulate, my former employer—all of them looked at me with sympathy but without belief. I was desperate, and it made me a little crazy. I picked up his picture, stroked his arm. "I'm just going to listen, like I had wished someone had done when you died. Save my place in line. This shouldn't take long."

"Diamond? Where are you? O'Rourke said you were the only one who could help me. You can't ignore me. I'm not going away." She laid on the damn doorbell again.

"Need to electrify that. Make people pay for disturbing me." In the small hallway, in the square connecting my back door, bedroom, bathroom, and kitchen, was a master control panel. One press of a button and the door she faced popped open.

"Listening isn't a promise to do anything else." I went to meet My Interruption. The back door led to a hallway shared by my living space and my working quarters. It was twenty feet long, wide enough for one person and a stack of boxes. Natural light filtered in through the bulletproof glass in the reinforced steel door at the end. On the other side, cast iron stairs connected the back entrance to the apartments, winding to the ground four floors below. Heeled shoes began to climb.

What was Irish doing sending this woman to me? I didn't do for-hire work, and he knew it.

Those heels were three floors below now. Blonde hair crested the black staircase. Blue eyes followed, her progress stopped as she scanned the landing above.

"Are you coming up or what? I have things to do."

"Are you planning to use that gun?" she asked suspiciously.

I looked down at the natural extension of my hand. "Nothing's out of the question."

"How good are you with it? On a scale of one to ten?"

A little smile grew despite my irritation. It was a good question. "I broke the scale. In or out?"

My Interruption studied my face. "In." Her heels clicked up the last of the stairs.

When she was on the landing, I stepped into her path. "Hands out. Turn around."

"You're patting me down?" She complied, muttering "ridiculous." "You're the one with the gun, you know."

Thorough is never ridiculous. "You got ten minutes." I went through the door, letting her follow. Or not. Her choice. I'd hear her out, connect her to people, to the help no one gave me. Fifteen minutes, twenty tops, and we'd be nothing to each other but a memory. "Nine minutes, forty-five seconds."

"My husband disappeared from work two days ago." She sat in the corner of the couch, knees together, fingers working the hem of her shirt. "He told his assistant he was going to lunch, then left alone, taking only his wallet and the book he was reading. When he didn't come home, I started looking for him."

Worry was evidenced by the purple tint underwriting her blue eyes. She hadn't been crying, not recently. Her eyes weren't swollen or red; her nose wasn't running or congested. No judgment there. Not everyone was a crier.

"This man who sent you, O'Rourke, how did you meet him?"

My Interruption rubbed the back of her neck. "The police, they are supposed to help, but no. I didn't know how to find the kind of help I needed." Her words had a subtle lilt. Something European perhaps? It was pleasant, slightly exotic, sounding as if every word was a secret. It added an unexpected twist to the cliché blonde hair, blue-eyed, buxom babe. "I found him on a message board. He met me at a café."

"When?"

She looked at her watch. "Two hours ago."

I had no doubt My Interruption met Irish—how else would she have my marker and address? But, four days ago, Irish and I said goodbye. He'd gotten a new assignment and was leaving town. Hasta la vista. Bon voyage. See ya when I see ya.

"Is something wrong?" she asked.

"No. Nothing. What did—" A smoke alarm interrupted the interrogation. "Hold that thought."

I bought this building six months before I "died." The front faced the busy main street. Six apartments on three floors. The back of the building had another set of six apartments looking over a parking lot to the cross street. All the apartments on the top floors were mine.

The smoke alarm came from the front building, the sound growing as I descended the stairs. Second floor, parking-lot side, resided the worst cook in the 202 area code. I pounded on the heavy door. "MaryAnn, it's Diamond." Not waiting for an invitation, I entered the bypass code that was part of my security upgrade. The lock slid open. I burst in and sprinted through the living and dining room to the kitchen.

"Stop that noise!" An irritated woman snapped a towel up at the blaring device.

The alarm mounted seven feet above the floor did not comply. Nor should it have.

"MaryAnn, your stove is on fire."

"Of course, it is," she shouted over the noise. "I'm making blackened chicken just like those Cajun chefs."

MaryAnn was a cooking channel enthusiast. Two months ago, I had fire extinguishers installed in all the kitchens after a marathon of barbecue episodes had the fire department here three times in one day. I set the gun I still carried by the sink, far away from the fire, pulled the extinguisher from its cradle, and snuffed the flames heading for the wall. Next, I opened her back door and retrieved the ladder stored in her common hallway for just this reason.

My eyeballs pulsed with the incessant noise. Hoping they wouldn't start bleeding, I set the ladder up, climbed, and all but ripped the fucker off the wall.

Silence was an ice cream cone after a late night at a rock concert.

"I don't know what happened." MaryAnn held a small butane torch in hand. "I was blackening the chicken when that damn thing went off. I did everything right, and it looks like I made charcoal. How do they make it look so easy?"

"They have a whole team." My Interruption had followed me down and was making herself useful by clearing the hot zone. "You only see one person in front of the camera, but three or four or more people actually figured out the recipe, doing all the practice runs without the film running."

"Is that how everything stays so clean? That's cheating. I'm MaryAnn McNamara."

"Hanna Lang," the woman formerly known as My Interruption said. "They use all kinds of tricks to make cooking look easy and appealing. It's their business."

MaryAnn pouted as she considered. "The lyin' dogs. Did any of my chicken survive?"

"Maybe this—"

I shook my head emphatically, clearing my throat to get Hanna's attention.

"—I'm sorry, no." Hanna got points for catching on. "It's a complete loss."

"Do you have any of the chef packaged meals?" I asked.

"You like those, and no open fire is required."

"Yes, I guess I could have one of those for dinner. It will give me time to make this recipe I found for dessert. Bananas Foster."

"No!" If I shouted, it wasn't unwarranted.

"Let's make dinner together," Hanna said, soothing MaryAnn. "It will be fun."

I scowled, my plans for a quick exit going up in smoke. I couldn't drag Hanna Lang out of the apartment without being subject to the McNamara Inquisition for the next week—wait. I didn't have a next week. "We were in the middle of a conversation. Hanna, the clock is still ticking."

"Of course. It was nice—" Hanna took a step to exit but was thwarted by a hand on her arm.

"You girls these days," MaryAnn said, pulling Hanna to the refrigerator. "Always in a hurry. No time for the niceties in life. When my Angus was with me..." MaryAnn talked about her dearly departed as she handed Hanna a packaged meal in a cute little bag. Next, MaryAnn went to the sink. I got a sponge, soap, and a bucket.

Hanna looked between me—the woman she was trying to hire—and an old woman with a proclivity for open flames.

Guess who lost.

I cleaned while Hanna and MaryAnn cooked. I worked quickly, trying to move the show along. It was a lost cause. The two clucked on like old friends meeting at a fence line. There was a silver lining. I was able to study Hanna Lang objectively, rooting out her secrets. Okay, MaryAnn did the rooting.

Hanna's family was from the fluid region where France and Germany abutted. She identified as German but had grown up with French cuisine. She came to the States, as we are generally known, ten months ago and was a post-doc candidate at my alma mater, Calvert College. She had one brother back in Germany. Both her parents were dead. The husband who was missing wasn't her husband but her almost fiancé. She was worried sick about him. He was a professor, an intellectual, a homebody.

"He was kidnapped. I know it," Hanna said. "He isn't rich. He isn't famous. He isn't anyone special except to me. He's my everything."

MaryAnn squeezed the younger woman's shoulder. "You'll do anything to get him back, won't you?"

"Yes, I will," Hanna answered solemnly, as if making a promise.

"Then that's what you'll do," MaryAnn said with certainty. "A woman can do extraordinary things for the man she loves. My Angus was a Scotsman to the bone. He worked twelve-hour days and made love to me every night. It was wrong for a man like that to get cancer. It would have taken away everything he was. A woman has to protect her man."

Hanna stilled, turning to squarely face MaryAnn. "She does. I didn't think men like my Damon existed. He is funny and so smart. He writes poems for me and reads them at poetry slams, open mic nights, friends' houses." She laughed softly, a tear spilling over her cheek. "He's not afraid to love me."

"Of course, he isn't. A man would have to be an idiot to be afraid to love a beautiful woman like you."

"Ah, but that is the trick. Men before wanted to own me. I was a thing, not a person. They may have loved the idea of me, but not me. The real me. I could shave my head and slice the skin from my face, and Damon would still want me."

MaryAnn blinked twice. "Maybe that didn't translate well, but I understand what you mean."

"This is ready. Do you have a plate?"

"Yes, unless Diamond extinguished them." MaryAnn opened a cabinet next to the sink, lifting three plates.

"None for us, MaryAnn." I pocketed the butane torch to thwart ideas of bananas Foster and anything flambé. "Hanna and I need to finish our conversation. Now. I have something to take care of tonight."

MaryAnn's shrewd eyes studied me, seeing more than I wanted. "You know how they always talk about it being darkest right before the storm?"

"Yes," I said with some caution, not sure where she was going.

"That is not the time to go running around naked."

Annnd, whaat? That is why I aspire to be an eccentric old woman.

I mean *aspired*.

MaryAnn's phone rang. I leapt at the interruption, literally, and pulled Hanna toward the front door. "No worries. I haven't run naked since I gave up tequila. Answer the phone. Bye-bye."

MaryAnn waved automatically, her mind already tuned to her caller. "Well, this is a surprise."

I shut the door behind us and ran up the stairs. Hanna followed me, up the stairs and back into my apartment. "It's obvious, she thinks the world of you."

It was a nice compliment as I thought the same of MaryAnn. But then, I have a soft spot for troublemakers. "People tend to do that when you keep their houses from burning down." A lump lodged in my throat. Who would be there for her the next time?

"It's more than that." Her intonation implied she saw through my bullshit. She cocked her head, her countenance becoming speculative. "She killed her husband, didn't she? Angus. She killed him before the cancer could."

I wasn't going to talk to a stranger about MaryAnn or anyone else in the building. "Let's talk about you. You aren't married. Not to Damon, if that's his real name, or to anyone else." I stood next to the door, arms crossed.

Hanna sank into the nearest chair. "No, we aren't married. But, really, why does that matter? He isn't any less missing because I'm his almost fiancée."

"If it didn't matter, why lie?"

"Because no one will help me." Exasperation pushed her back to her feet. She paced as she talked, her hands punctuating the sentences. "Ugh, I hate this. Why does a commitment have to be printed on paper and signed to be real? I don't need a ring or a dress or a cake. I love him. He loves me. That should be enough."

"Tell me the story, from the start. Zero lies, no bullshit."

She took a deep breath as she walked the longest path across a relatively small room. "I moved here last summer after I was accepted into the graduate program at the college. I worked for a year after finishing university at home. I am a psychologist, but without advanced degrees, I wasn't much more than a glorified assistant. I didn't have the money to go to school, but my brother said he would help. It was...the best day." A smile graced the serious set of her mouth. A good memory. "I submitted my application and was accepted. I sold everything I had. It was more frightening than I expected. I was used to living alone, but things are different here. Classes started. When I wasn't working, I studied in a café in a bookstore. I liked the people there—"

"Stop." This is the problem. Whenever you tell somebody to tell you the whole story, they go far, far beyond what you need to know. "Tell me about this kidnapping. Not your life story."

"Oh. Sorry." She blew out a deep breath and started again in this century. "From what I've been able to piece together, Damon left for lunch two days ago and hasn't been seen or heard from since. He left alone, carried nothing but his wallet and a book. He never made it to the restaurant."

"No one is concerned. Is there a reason?"

"People are concerned, just not ones wearing badges. The police won't look because Damon's assistant got an email, supposedly from him, saying he needed some time to think and would be back in a few days."

"So, someone has heard from him."

She slapped her hands on her thighs. "He would have told me. *Me*. Not his assistant. Not his supervisor. Me. Damon is a planner. He didn't make out a grocery list without talking it over. He would not leave for a 'few days' without talking it through three times. He just wouldn't." She shook her head in defeat. "You don't believe me either."

Something scratched at my front door. "I'm collecting facts.

I'm not to the 'believe or disbelieve' point yet," I said, unlocking the door still being scratched. "What the hell is going on out here?" A dozen puppies invaded my house. Twelve times twenty pounds of yips, yaps, and yelps. "Whoa. Stop. Son of a bitch."

Hanna cooed. "They're so cute."

"Catch them." I captured the last one, too tubby to keep up with his brothers and sisters. The butane torch dug into my belly. The torch went from my pocket to a high bookshelf. "Su-Chen!" I hung over the banister, glaring at the open door of apartment 3A. "Su-Chen, they escaped again." Tubbo began bathing my face with his little puppy tongue.

It may or may not have gotten in my mouth.

In my apartment, Hanna sat on the floor, attracting four of the canines. She crooned in German as they climbed over each other for her attention. Being part shepherd, they wagged their tails harder.

"Take Tubbo," I said, dropping the largest pup into her lap. "Where did the others go?"

"I don't know."

"I see you! Don't go under the table." I caught one little foot just before it disappeared under a chair. Two split the difference, running out on either side of me. It was the classic choice of a bird in the hand versus two in the bush. I kept the one I had, running on my knees after the others.

Su-Chen Wong came in with Blossom, the puppy momma, both of whom seemed entertained by the chaos. "I so sorry, Diamond."

Doubted it. I've seen Su-Chen sorry. Regret didn't make her eyes sparkle.

"I don't know how they get out."

Didn't buy it either. Only one mammal in the apartment had opposable thumbs.

"Come pup-pups. You come now."

Shockingly, the pup-pups did not obey. One did squat and pee. Then a second ran through the puddle, leaving a trail of paw prints into my kitchen.

"Get a box," I ordered. "Or a basket. Something."

Hanna ran past me, a train of fluff followed. "Got one!" She came back in, carrying my laundry basket filled with her entourage. "They're heavy."

I added the one I caught. "Keep them in there. Su-Chen, grab the one on the couch." I lunged for a little one making a break for it. "Two more."

Su-Chen cleaned the floor while she gave the apologies I knew she didn't mean. I herded the last two, leaving Hanna to guard against more prison breaks.

I deposited the last in the basket. "I thought you found homes for them."

"Yes, for most. Two more weeks, then Blossom will be ready."

Right, because it was Blossom who couldn't give up the pups.

Su-Chen stroked the bitch's regal head. "You should take one. Be good company for you. Since my husband died, my Blossom is my companion."

"Su-Chen, we talked about this. It's not possible."

"All things possible," she said over my objection. "The big one. He like you."

"No." I hoped simple and direct would work. "I'll carry the basket of escape artists down for you."

Su-Chen ignored me, turning her attention to Hanna, who was kissing the head of one. "Lily like you. You take her home, she be a good guard."

"She's adorable...but I can't have a dog. Maybe someday."

I picked up the really heavy, awkward basket. It was the only way to get back to our regularly scheduled program. Su-Chen and Blossom followed. After depositing all of them in her living room, I climbed the stairs to get back to business.

"They really are adorable," Hanna said when I returned.

Sure, they were. They were puppies. "Next time, they can piss on your floor. Now, where were we?"

The glow of puppies faded. "I don't know if the message was

faked or he was coerced into sending it. I just know Damon would not have left town without talking it through with me."

"You said the police thought there was another woman?"

"The one *potential* sighting of him was with a woman. They met outside a parking garage and then went in together. It wasn't him. He doesn't have a car, and he already has a woman. Me. I think she kidnapped him."

"He went with her willingly?" When she shrugged, I pressed on. "Has there been a ransom? Any demands made?"

Thunder rolled up the front stairs. What the fuck was going on tonight? Was it a full moon or something? I threw the door open, ready to slap down whatever stupid crisis was coming next.

"Diamond!" One hundred eighty pounds of teen hit me hard, carrying me across my living room and plastering me to the wall. Andrew Dixon's arms wrapped tight, stealing my breath.

"Dix, what the fuck?" I grabbed his shoulders, trying to make some space. That's when I realized he was crying.

"You're not dead. You're not dead." Dixon repeated the mantra into my shoulder. I felt his relief. Guilt spread over me, hot as fire. It burned away the annoyance and irritation I'd been running on, leaving me to choke on the cinders.

"Not dead." I cleared my throat, trying to get my voice back. "Not yet. Squeeze any harder and a rib might pop out though." I chuckled, inviting him to do the same.

"Sorry." With no trace of humor, he pulled his weight off me. We had some awkward body contact going on. He wasn't ready to let go but struggled with touching.

Knowing he had good reason for both, I wove my arm around his waist, putting his front to my side and looking into a face on the verge of manhood. Dixon escaped an abusive home and now lived in one of my penthouse apartments. He was the best mix of black and Asian. His skin tone was light for a black man, dark for an Asian. His features were broad and strong, his eyes almond-shaped and dark. His black hair hung pin-straight past his chin, always hiding the left side of his face. He was creeping up on six foot but seemed taller for his long, slender arms and legs. I squeezed his waist, pulling him tight against me. "Nothing happened."

Ian Black stood on my threshold, his expression something I couldn't name. Concern? Anxiety? Anger? He didn't soften, seeing me imitating a pancake. Just an hour ago, he and Dixon had finished a pizza, then left for a movie. If it wasn't for Hanna, the fire alarm, and a puppy stampede, this scene would have been very different.

It was almost as if he knew.

Ian noticed the statuesque blonde for the first time. His expression transformed from *I'm-gonna-kill-you* to *Hello-baby*. "I'm Ian. Ian Black. And you are?"

"Hanna Lang. I'm hiring Diamond to find my fiancé. He's been kidnapped."

Ian walked into the room with the confidence of a man who could sell sin to a nun. "You'll have to forgive Diamond. She likes to brag about her brains, but she's underfunded in the manners department." He pulled a card from his wallet and offered it. "As Diamond's business partner, we accept the job." He held on when she accepted the card, making for a cringy moment of tug-of-war.

"Dix, run down to the driveway and get my bathroom screen. Casanova, can I talk to you? Privately?" I caught a fistful of Ian's shirt as I walked by, dragging his ass into the kitchen. "I don't do for hire."

Ian was the most forgettable man alive. He'd never be mistaken for handsome, but he wasn't ugly. Ugly people are memorable. Ian was not. He was average height with average coloring on an average build. Thoroughly uninteresting. Don't feel bad for Ian. He banked on being overlooked in a crowd. Away from the five foot seven Barbie doll, Ian was back to scowling. That ordinary man paced away from me, stopping in the little hall, ignoring me.

"I said I don't do for hire."

Ian had talents that people relied on. He could get anything, anywhere, at any time. I called him a purveyor. People. Weapons. Connections. Intelligence. We had been professional acquaintances during my CIA days. We weren't acquaintances anymore. I thought we were friends, but as he turned, fire blazing in those common brown eyes, the look on his face said I was wrong.

"What were you doing tonight?" The question wasn't innocent. He looked away from me, into my bathroom.

"I…" What was there to say? In the face of his anger, I defaulted to the lame-ass answer of every kid. "Nothing."

He pulled a gun from his jacket pocket and set it on the counter. It was my gun, the one I carried into MaryAnn's kitchen. In my hurry, I had forgotten it. I'd been caught in the act of many things over my life. This was the only time I was speechless.

"Whatever is going on in that fucked-up head of yours, get this straight: it isn't happening." Ian never lost his cool. He was too experienced. When we worked together, he always followed my lead. He never led, always followed. His chin up, arms crossed over his thin chest, he was changing the rules. "Take the job."

I swallowed hard. When I spoke, it was with authority. "We'll listen. We'll figure out what she needs and get her help, but I'm not going to take the job." I rubbed a year-old ache, the spot where my heart used to beat. "The last thing I need is someone else's problems."

Ian covered my hand with his. "You aren't doing this alone."

"Dixon will—" Then I noticed it. Our hands were pressed over my heart. And the dots connected. "You called them. MaryAnn's chicken. Su-Chen's puppies."

"Somewhere in the middle of the previews, it clicked. I knew what you were planning. I called Su-Chen, then MaryAnn. She told me about the fire and Hanna. I'm so mad at you right now, I could choke you, but I'm not going to. Instead, we're going back in there and listening to what that woman has to say." He shoved me through the door, forcing me to return to the living room.

Hanna stood, her posture awkward. She was uncomfortable. I couldn't blame her, not with the carnival that was the last hour.

"Our apologies," he said, with bullshit manners. "Family matters. Why don't we sit down?"

Door crash. Slam. Refrigerator door.

Buurrrrpppp.

Dix was back. "How'd that get down there, Diamond?"

I cut him off. "To recap, your boyfriend-slash-fiancé left work two days ago for lunch. He didn't arrive at his destination. There was a message sent to his assistant saying he was leaving town for a few days and a report that he met another woman."

"But those are wrong," Hanna argued to the new faces in the room. "Damon isn't a spontaneous man, and he isn't a cheater. If he left town, it was because he was forced to. He..." She pressed her tongue to her upper lip, stopping her wayward words.

"There's no point holding something back," Ian said. "What Diamond doesn't find out, Dixon will."

Dix flashed an Oscar-worthy smile.

Hanna cocked her head at the curiosity that was my head of IT and Mischief. "His research grant is through the U.S. Army. He is an expert in chemical deterrents. What he was working on was revolutionary. Maybe somebody took him for what's in his head. They don't want money. They want him."

Sam Irish, the sneaky bastard, sent me the one case he thought I couldn't walk away from. Hanna's story mirrored my own with one big exception: her man wasn't dead. Not yet. Not that she knew. No matter what I did or didn't do for her, my husband would remain dead and buried.

There was no upside for me.

And I hated being managed.

"If you're right," I said in my calmest, most professional voice, "then contact the Army. They have the resources to find your man." I crossed to the front door, opened it. "Good luck. I really hope you find him."

"I need you to find him. You." When I shook my head, she ruthlessly turned her blue eyes on Ian. "I have money. I can pay. Ten thousand. I can get more. Damn it. His name is Dr. Damon Marten. He's a professor at Calvert College. His life matters."

Shut the front door.

Boys and girls, life just got interesting.

HOW TO MAKE AN ASS USING YOU AND ME

Recently, I read an article that argued coincidences are not the unique and eerie events they seem to be. Instead, they're the ordinary result of living in a world that just isn't that big. Statistically speaking. Putting the internet article into practice, there was nothing noteworthy about Sam Irish sending a stranger to my door on the very day I was going to check out.

And, natch, the stranger would be a female desperate to find her man, one the police did not believe was the victim of foul play.

And that man would be a professor using his big brain for good.

And that professor would be the same who was *my* advisor in college and instrumental in helping me land my dream job with the CIA.

Coincidence, my left ass cheek.

"Cut the bullshit." I whipped the words at Hanna, intentionally stinging to get attention. "Who do you work for? Al-Qaeda? Taliban? Libya? Iran?" With each naming of a U.S. foe, I stepped forward and she stepped back, a stop-frame demonstration of the predator-and-prey relationship.

Now, I didn't actually think she worked for one of these organizations. If she did, she wouldn't be here trying to buy my services. But she wasn't coming close to telling me the whole truth. "*My husband's missing, I mean my fiancé, actually my boyfriend.* Your relationship downgraded faster than a hurricane."

To get the truth, I needed Miss Hanna Lang to be more afraid of me than whoever she was covering for. I straightened, walked away, giving her space to think about her story. "It's better if you tell me yourself than if I have to"—dramatic pause—"extract it."

She pressed her hand to her throat in dramatic feminine insult. "What? No. No, no, no." With each denial, she retreated until her back was against the wall. "You're nuts. A lunatic." Her eyes went to Ian. He looked to me, silently picking my side. Hanna got the message. It was my way or the highway. "I don't need you. I'll find him myself." She pushed off the wall, snagged her purse, then made for the door. "You seriously need therapy."

Exit Hanna Lang.

The three of us stood in my living room, listening to the footfalls race down the stairs.

Ian moved to the front window watching, I assume, Hanna's ass—I mean exit. "What the hell, Diamond?"

"Me? What was with the Romeo routine?"

"I was being supportive of our client."

"Supportive, my ass. Whatever. That was the opening move in a sucker's game. She'll be back." I sat on the arm of my couch. "This is no simple job. Damon Marten and I have history. Somebody is using Hanna Lang to get to me to find him. Irish is the obvious answer. He sent her here. Why did he take the meet with Hanna in the first place? Why did he send her to me, calling in a priceless IOU?"

Ian shook his head. "I've never trusted him."

"If Irish is in the game, there's an angle. No doubt." Truer words were never spoken. My heart raced, my muscles fired in anticipation of action.

What the hell. Dying could wait a day. It was game on. "Ready for your assignments?"

Dixon may have stayed quiet during the drama, but he was all-in now. "Sweet! Tell me what you need."

"Everything about Dr. Damon Marten, Ph.D. I've been out of touch with him for a few years, but my system will have his contact information. Damon didn't have a life outside of work so, as Hanna suggested, we start with his work life." As my Chief Information Ferret, Dixon could get in any data crevice. He'd been hacking since he was twelve. He'd been caught and ended up in a program unfortunately named the Youth Prevention Facility, where I worked as a positive influence to give structure to brilliant but undisciplined minds. "I want you to get everything and break it down, just like you did with Gavriil, then we'll go through it together. Get everything on Hanna Lang, too. I want to know her secrets and if our client can afford us."

"You need anything from me?" Ian asked.

Ian didn't have Dixon's binary skills but was unparalleled in connections. "Check if there are any orders out for Marten. Find me a lead."

"Right. Kid, I need a picture of our man. Get one of the woman, too. What are you going to do, Diamond?"

"I'm going back to school."

Welcome to Calvert College, my alma mater. I'm legacy. The man my mother denies is my father graduated from here. His father, too. I had the grades and the scores to get into any school, but Calvert was the only place I wanted to go.

Damon taught the chemistry course and lab mandatory for all college of science freshman. My lab partner changed to the business college after two weeks, which left me on my own with all those compounds and vials and heat. Unlike MaryAnn McNamara, my flames created. After the fire department finished their lecture, we discovered a heat-resistant material, which led to a grant that doubled the size of the chemistry department's lab facilities.

Damon volunteered to keep an eye on me, but I knew it was his way of getting me to transfer from physics to the small-but-cutting-edge chemistry department. Damon was my advisor, my employer, and my inside connection to the bigger world.

The much bigger world.

Parking in a half-empty lot, I thumbed through my contacts and hit send. A computerized voice didn't bother with greeting me. "Leave your message."

Beep.

"Irish, it's Diamond. What's the deal with Hanna Lang? I don't know what game you're playing, but I'm not touching it until I hear from you."

Irish would return my call. Eventually. Until then, I'd just see for myself what Damon had been up to.

It was nearly nine o'clock, but this close to the summer solstice, campus was still bright and bustling. People of all shapes, sizes, and colors strolled along walkways separating cultured gardens. Some things never change.

It had been years since I'd been on campus, but I couldn't risk being recognized. My short dark hair was hidden beneath a long blonde wig, the style common among twenty-somethings. Contacts changed my green eyes to blue. I dressed in light layers with the tools of my trade concealed between them.

The front doors of the chemistry building were unlocked. I walked confidently through them, acting as though I belonged, expecting I was being picked up by some hidden camera. The center hall gave me three options. To either side were the north and south wings of the first floor. Directly in front was the triple-wide stairway to the three floors above.

It had been nine years since I wore the cap and gown. Funny what had changed and what hadn't. The faculty list was displayed on a bright LED screen, split with scrolling ads for campus events and cheap food. Of the list itself, I recognized all but one professor. The department chair from my days had earned the tag "emeritus," and the reviled O-chem professor was now in charge. Little changes. Updates that kept up with the times but didn't try to get ahead of them.

Damon's office was in the same spot. Third floor, front corner. Next door was the department chair's office. Both were accessed through an anteroom where the administrative assistant for the department sat.

The door was locked.

A quick scan convinced me the upgrades to the early twentieth-century building hadn't included surveillance of this hallway. With the work of a minute, I stood in the efficient space of a tidy woman who had a peculiar thing for cows. The one on the poster behind her desk had a particularly disapproving look.

Relocking the door, I went behind the desk and booted the computer. As the lights flickered, I called Dixon. "I'm plugging into the admin's computer now." I attached an ordinary-looking thumb drive. "Let me know when you're connected."

"It's thinking," he said into my earpiece. "Are you going to the store tomorrow?"

"Wasn't planning on it."

"But we're out of everything. I'm surviving on peanut butter and jelly tacos." He took a bite, a big bite. "'U don' wan' me wastin' to nuffin, do u?"

"If it means you never chew in my ear again, I'm good with starving you."

Pause. Swallow. "Sorry. I'm connected."

"I'm moving into the office." I would have to grocery shop. Being as today was to be my last day on this planet, I let my cupboard run down to nil. My stomach growled, complaining that the kitchen wasn't the only thing empty.

The door was closed to Damon's office, but it wasn't locked. I stepped into the middle of the L-shaped room. To my left was the same U-shaped desk I remembered, but the wood guest chairs had been replaced with modern versions complete with padding. To my right was a table with three chairs facing a wall-mounted whiteboard. Any wall space that didn't have a window had a bookcase. The titles were readable in the waning daylight, allowing me to keep the lights off.

My priority was his computer, which did not sit on his desk. Or under it. A quick check of the desk drawers found my quarry. I booted the laptop, inserted the second thumb drive, and alerted Dixon.

"I see it," he said. "Download has started."

"Good." While technology did its thing, I went through Damon's office, looking for clues to his current project. The papers on his desk were stacked in neat piles. The first pile was a hard-copy draft of a graduate student's paper. The red notations ended two pages in. A work in progress.

The second stack was a hard-copy print of a textbook in revision. Damon was a contributing author to chapters on exothermic reactions.

The third stack was technical journals. The nine magazines were flagged by Post-it notes.

"Useless."

I sat in his chair and began going through his desk files. Second drawer, I found an eight-by-ten photo of Damon with Hanna Lang. It was taken without their knowledge by a long-distance lens. "Found a picture, surveillance type."

"Blackmail? Did they get busted doing something?"

"No. It's just a picture." They were a study in opposites. Her light skin, his dark. Her hair long, his cropped short. She, stylish and sophisticated; he, wrinkled and off-the-rack. Damon's arms were around Hanna, her head thrown back in laughter. The look on his face was unmistakable.

What they were to each other didn't need a label. It was real. The corners of the photo were worn from frequent handling.

A click came from the outer office. It was a small sound made enormous in the space where it didn't belong. The turning of a locked knob. "I got company."

"Get out of there! Hurry. Diamond, you need to get out." The panic in his young voice was diametrically opposed to the feeling thrumming through my body. Small, light scratches of metal on metal were fingernails on a chalkboard in the silent room.

"Shhh. I'm good. You just finish these downloads." I closed the office door. Locked it to buy another minute. I relocated the laptop to a low bookshelf, below natural eye level, disguising it amid ten pounds of textbooks while Dixon's gadget raped its mind.

I surveyed the room. Hiding wasn't an option, so I guessed it was going to be fighting.

Who am I kidding, it was always going to be fighting.

The professor's office held a plethora of odd keepsakes that could be considered weapons in the right hands. Fortunately for me, I had the right hands. Two right hands. I rearranged a bit, tipping the feng shui in my favor.

"Diamond? Are you still there?"

The outer lock opened. Two entered.

"Shhh." It was the only response he would get. He needed reassurance, I got that, but I needed silence. No one but me may be able to hear Dixon, but my uninvited guests would be listening for unexpected sounds.

Damon's door was tried. I pulled a bull penis cane from a wall mounting. A light touch persuaded the lock to open. A professional hand. The door swung quickly to ninety degrees. A profile entered the room. I swung low. The bull penis cane snapped smartly across shin bones. My opponent somersaulted, grunting as momentum took him across the office floor. I followed with the cane, landing a blow to the shoulders, then a second, a third before it snapped. A limp cock being useless to a woman, I tossed it aside. My opponent was down. Never one to take things at face value, I palmed a crystal paperweight. I slam-dunked that bitch, but the trajectory of a geode was disrupted by a well-placed ceramic guernsey. Quartz and cow parts exploded into skin-shearing fractals, announcing the entrance of my second visitor.

Instinct made me duck, saving me from the ass-kicker boot aimed at my head. Then it was kick, jab, block, knee, spin, kick, block, moon rock, uppercut, terracotta warrior (miniature), front kick, bicycle (full-sized), side kick, front kick, gun.

“Enough, bitch.” The woman aiming a gun at my left breast was all the more pissed for having udders projecting from between, well, her udders. “Diamond? Is that you?”

“Trixie? I knew I recognized those moves.” I planted my hands on my thighs and assumed a gasping runner’s pose. I was grateful it was Trixie. She and I used to run in the same circles. She was a thief. Sometimes she worked for the good guys, including me. Other times, not. “You always did have a mean kick.”

“Thanks. You’ve lost some of your moves. Your edge is as dull as peanut butter, but I liked what you did with the dick stick. Did you have to be so hard on Ruthie? She’s still in training.”

My jaw was on the tiled floor. Lost my moves? Peanut butter?

She did not just get ugly.

She checked her partner, tapping the woman’s cheek. “Heard you retired, became one of those Real Housewives of Suburbia USA. What happened to pull you out?”

I got back in character. “Some fucker killed my husband.”

Her head snapped toward me, eyes filled with lethal intent. “You need help?”

Trixie was her own brand of lethal. The offer meant a lot. She was good people. “Taken care of, but thanks. On to the next thing. What are you doing here?”

“Same as you, looking to cash in on the prize for finding Poe’s raven. I assumed it wouldn’t be as easy as being in the guy’s office, but it was worth a look.”

Since I had no idea what she was talking about, I nodded. Damon had an interest in Edgar Allan Poe that bordered on obsessive. He was a sucker for every trinket and novelty related to the poet and his work. The raven was one of his favorite images. “You know what they say about assuming.”

“Exactly.” We turned our attention to the room, managing to still keep an eye on each other. Soon, four ravens were deposited on the table. A framed print. A ceramic raven. A black wire raven. An unframed oil painting.

The framed print was dismantled. It was an ornate gold,

something that would have belonged a hundred years ago. Being made of a modern resin, it was light, a fraction of the weight of wood. The print was simply that. A mass-market production of ink on paper. Behind it was cardboard giving the depth needed for the frame, then the frame stand. In short: nothing.

The ceramic raven held its head high and wings wide. The moment before flight. The bottom was stamped "Made in China." It was hollow, and something rattled within. Trixie picked a chunk of geode from the floor and smashed the bird. We sorted through the chards, finding more nothing.

We didn't bother with the wire raven. The metal was coiled into the shape of the bird, but it wasn't solid. You could see through it from every angle. The shape contained equal amounts of air and nothing.

I pulled out a switchblade knife and flicked it open.

"Thanks for not using that before," Trixie said. She took a similar but smaller version from her boot. Together we dissected the oil painting. I didn't know what we were looking for, so my attention was on Trixie. While she had skills enough to be a top operative, she chose to specialize. She called herself an "acquirer of fine goods." Like I said, she was a thief. Art, jewels, money, show tickets, haute couture. The woman didn't slum. She was sought-after because she was exacting, as she was now, working methodically to peel each painted black feather from the bird.

"How's business?" I asked.

Shortly before I retired, Trixie formed a company, transforming from an independent contractor to an entrepreneur. She smiled, never looking up from her work. "Never better. Offer still stands. Anytime you're ready, I got a place for you."

I returned the friendly rapport. "In case you hadn't heard, I've got issues with authority. If I worked for you, you'd be my boss. I'd hate your orders; you'd hate my lip. One thing would lead to another and before you know it, there's blood on the floor."

"True, but being a good boss, I'd sew you back together

before I sent you out on your next job. I like to think of myself as a benevolent overlord." She straightened. "It's not here. No other ravens?"

We both looked around. It was a small space. Took five seconds.

Trixie planted her feet, squared her shoulders. "I'm taking the computer."

"Nope," I said, rolling onto the balls of my feet. "I called dibs."

And then it was all jab, block, uppercut, dodge, picture frame, kick, catch, flip, elbow. I stepped on the human rug named Ruthie, losing my balance. Trixie aimed her fist for my head, caught the bookcase. "Damn it. God damn it."

I buried my boot in her gut, doubled her over, then leapt into the outer office.

Trixie filled the doorway, one hand holding onto the frame. "What are you up to?"

"Today's forecast calls for rain." I pulled the fire alarm.

The siren blared.

"Bitch!" Trixie said, or at least that's what I thought she said. I couldn't hear anything over the monotone shrieking of the alarm. She raced back to the human rug, hefting the junior woman over her shoulder. "Think about the job offer, Diamond. Call me, we'll do lunch!" she shouted as she plowed past me.

"I will." I stayed put, waiting until she disappeared down the staircase. They were precious seconds, but she was just the kind to double back. I snagged the laptop off the shelf and beat it out of there. Dixon's gadget had gone dark, meaning I already owned this bitch. Still, I wasn't going to leave it for the next vulture to pick over, especially when I didn't know the game. I made like a running back with the ball as orders from the first responders came from the main stairway. I went left, past Damon's lab to the grad student hallway. My old office was unlocked and empty. I put the old adage into effect, closing the door then opening a window. I slipped the laptop into my jacket, zipped it, but still had to press my arm against it to keep it in place.

Out the window, the decorative stone shelf had shrunk since I was an undergrad. Ten steps got me to the corner; one leap and I was on the fire escape. Third floor. Second floor. The last section was suspended a dozen feet above the ground, meant to make sure cheaters, ne'er-do-wells, and other forms of trouble used the front door. My weight would tip the balance, lower the section, and float me to the ground like a feather.

That was the theory.

Reality was less fluid. The damn thing wouldn't move.

Sirens roared from another fire truck as I moved my weight out. The pulley denied me. I bounced. The pulley screeched, yelling at me. I swore back. "You good-for-nothing piece of shit! That is a fire. You're my escape. Get in the fucking game."

And then it did.

Gravity had me sliding painfully down steps meant for walking. Both hands dug in, grappling for anything to stop my fall. My left hand caught, my ass and legs kept going. The laptop dropped like a rock. My heart raced from the scare. Served me right. Bet you half of Irish's Swiss stash that I was the last person to use this ladder, and that was ten years ago.

I let go, sticking the landing three feet below. I bent down to the soft patch where the laptop landed. "Come to Mama."

"Freeze!" White light blinded me. "Stand up, slowly, hands where I can see them."

STOP ME IF YOU'VE HEARD THIS ONE

Deputy Dawg stood over me, his flashlight both a tool and a weapon. I couldn't see beyond the bright white light burning my retinas. I spoke quickly, giving him something more important to handle than little ol' me. "Call nine-one-one." I climbed to my feet, gasping as though I just escaped a fire. "There's...there's a fire on the third floor. It's bad."

A strong hand helped me to standing. "Fire department's en route. What were you doing on the fire escape?"

"Escaping the fire." The *duh* went unsaid.

"Do I know you?" The light circled back over my face. "Naw. It can't be...Annalisa? But I thought..."

First reaction: bite the head off the SOB stupid enough to use that name. Second reaction: the voice sounded familiar. "Trevor?" I held my palm out, blocking the beam. "Stop blinding me and let me see your skinny face."

Instantly, the stream of light was replaced with a glow of a lantern. Still unnaturally white, it now cast hard-edged shadows that illuminated the grinning face of Trevor Hargrove. "Still sneaking out the back? Were you in a fight?" The crow's feet at his eyes appeared when he smiled. "Some things never change."

For logistical reasons, a university police annex had been constructed on the backside of the chemistry building. Trevor and I met my freshman year. He was a rookie officer assigned to all the shit duties, which often had him working out of the poorly equipped outpost. He'd been gangly then, his torso too narrow for his height. That wasn't the case anymore.

"Something told me today wasn't going to be ordinary. Come on, trouble, you know the way."

Trevor escorted me into the small office, then left me on my own recognizance to check on the situation three floors up. I had the laptop and considered slipping out, but a university police lieutenant just might have information I could use. Having time to kill, I got comfortable in Trevor's executive-grade chair and checked in with Dixon. It was only then that I realized my earpiece was gone. Damn it. I dialed, pissed that I'd lost it. That one was a good fit, finally. The phone rang once.

"You're alive!"

"Of course, I am. Dix, you gotta learn to have confidence in my skills." I kept it light, giving space for his blood pressure to return to its natural orbit. "It was kinda fun. Turned out to be an old friend."

"Okay. That's good, I guess. We got it all, Diamond. I'm already running an algorithm to sort the emails."

"Nice. Is it turning up anything?" I had time, and Dix needed the conversation. I understood about ten percent of what he said. After living with Gavriil for years, I'd perfected the art of interested-sound injection into conversation.

Eventually, he ran out of acronyms and slang to throw at me. "Are you on your way home?"

"Soon. I made a contact here and am going to see what he knows. It's going to delay me an hour. I need to talk to Ian."

"Okay...IAN. DIAMOND WANTS TO TALK TO YOU."

"Ah, fuck." I jerked my arm, putting distance between his screaming voice and my bleeding ear. "Damn it, Dixon."

"Diamond?" Ian's voice was small coming from arm's length away. "You there?"

I opted for speakerphone. "Yeah, I'm here. Deaf, but present."

"What's going on?"

"I had a little company tonight. Trixie and her trusty sidekick joined in."

"The Cleaning Ladies? Holy fuck, Diamond, what is this professor into?"

"That's what we need to find out. And fast. Someone is putting up real money for a raven. Damon was obsessed with Edgar Allan Poe. She said there is a cash prize for Poe's raven. There were four in the office. We took them apart and didn't find a thing."

"Well, it gives me something to work with. I put feelers out and am waiting on answers." He exhaled noisily. "Having the Cleaning Ladies show up takes this to another level."

"It implies that whoever put up the cash does not have Damon Marten." Behind me, the door creaked as it opened. "Need to run. Follow the money. Find me that bird."

Trevor came in, shooing me out of the good chair, dropping his hat on a nail doing duty as a hook. "Sorry to keep you waiting."

I made my way to the visitor side of the desk. "Fire under control?"

"False alarm. You wouldn't know anything about that, would you?" He settled into his chair, not pushing back on the innocent look I carefully wore. "Wondered if you'd be here when I got back. Half convinced myself I saw a ghost."

"I am a ghost, in a way." It was that déjà vu feeling as I settled into his creaky guest chair. "It's been a long time since we've done this but seems like just yesterday."

"It does." He laughed, easy and relaxed, then pulled open a low file drawer and set a manila file on the desk. My maiden name was written across the top in thick, black letters. "Your eyes are blue."

"They are tonight." I flipped the file open. "I go by Diamond now." On the top was my obituary.

"And you're dead?"

I gave him the back-of-the-book version. One night in Rome. One car. One dead scientist. Italian police investigate, but in the end, all they have are kind words for the new widow. Months later, a video emerges challenging the facts. Had he stepped into traffic, or was he pushed? The widow returns to the police, where there are more kind words but no answers. Exit the widow.

Enter Diamond. My widow's run unearths a plethora of suspects: the small-time crook, the mule-loving rancher, the lady in waiting, the Russian bookseller, the soon-to-be priest. Following the stink that greed leaves in its wake reveals big lies and ugly truths. "Murder is filthy business. Good thing I like playing dirty." I leaned toward him. "Being dead and all, I need you to keep this little visit between us."

He snorted. "Some things really never do change."

I turned the page in his file on me. There it was, the first case report. It was the fire in Damon's lab. "Wasn't my fault, you know."

"Denial always was your strong suit. Diamond." His gaze slid over me, trying it on for size. He shook his head as though laughing at some inside joke. "Okay, *Diamond*, what were you doing upstairs?"

"I heard Damon is missing. Came to check it out for myself."

"Were you in his office? His lab?"

"His office. The door was unlocked. It hasn't changed much since I graduated. Some new toys on the shelves."

"Most of them are broken now. Looks like a fight happened in there."

I cocked my head. "Thought you said it was a fire?"

He mirrored me. "You said it was a fire."

And there we stayed.

Five seconds later, I redirected. "I heard he went out for lunch and didn't come back. The official line is he took some time off. Voluntarily. Are you buying it?"

Trevor hesitated, lagging just enough to tell me he had something to say on the matter. His mouth stayed shut.

"Damon and I kept in touch over the years. He helped get me the job with the feds. I met him after I finished those first months of training, when I was eager to take on the world. Then again whenever I was in town and our schedules worked out. A few years ago, my life went a different direction. I didn't call as much as I should have, but I never stopped caring. My work took me around the world and gave me a unique set of skills that I've used to make a difference in people's lives. The least I can do is the same for the man who saw something worth keeping in that girl who set his lab on fire." If that didn't loosen his lips, I would have to break out the WD-40.

Trevor straightened my file, then closed the cover. He put it back in the drawer, taking another file out. This one he held on his lap. "How much did Damon tell you about his work before he came to Calvert?"

"Not much. I know he did post-grad work abroad. He talked about taking trains between the countries and the different cities he'd been to. He didn't talk about his work. What did he tell you?"

"About four months ago, he came across an *in memoriam* in one of his journals." Trevor set the file on the desk and opened it. He flipped pages over until he came to a one-page article on a scientist named Knoll Klemer. The thirty-six-year-old chemical engineer had been named a top-forty-under-forty the previous year. "He drowned in the Seine two days after he emailed Damon saying they needed to talk. Then, two months ago, Monica Hass jumped off the roof of the ten-story building where she worked."

My heart shifted into second gear. "Let me guess, she also contacted him?"

"She did."

"Who was she to Damon?"

"He called both of them colleagues. She warned him people were after the work they did in Germany. She worked for the German government and had reached out to her other channels. Damon loved talking about his work, but this..." He shook his head. "All he would say was 'We were young.' Being closed-lipped concerned me. He said she was going into hiding and advised him to do the same."

"You think he went into hiding."

"I hope he did, but I don't know. Damon has come here a few times a week for years. He bought gifts when my kids were born. He's my friend, and the last thing I'm going to do is get him killed by helping God knows who find him."

I nodded, supporting, understanding. "What if he's not in hiding? What if *they* got him?"

"I've thought of that, but I don't know who to trust. And I can't be the reason he ends up dead."

"You trust me, right? You know Damon trusts me."

He sat, quietly staring at me. "I did. But that was a long time ago."

I tried a different angle. "Have you met Hanna Lang? What do you think of her?"

"I've met her but can't say I know her. She moved into his house a few months ago. He's in deep with her. My impression was if someone was after him, he didn't want her getting hurt by proximity."

"You think that's why he just walked away midday? To provide some distance and, thereby protection, for Hanna? Why not just take her with him?"

Trevor shrugged. "Maybe he couldn't."

I flipped through the file. It contained printed articles on the deceased scientists and little else. Still, it was a starting point. "Can I make a copy of these?"

"Sure, they're public information." He pointed me to the copier. "Are you going to look for him?"

"Yes, but not haphazardly." I set the small stack into the feeder and let the machine work. "First, I need to understand what this history is that has two of his colleagues dead. If I'm lucky, that will point me to who's after Damon. Once the threat is neutralized, I can find our friendly neighborhood chemistry professor and get him back to his classroom."

"I like that plan. Let him stay hidden until we secure the scene. What can I do to help?"

"I'd like to see his lab." I smile, inviting him to play. "Preferably with the lights on."

"Let's go. The fire department has left. I'll just hold onto this." He took Damon's laptop from my side of the desk.

I shrugged as though it was no big deal, because it wasn't. "Lock it up tight and don't let anyone know it's here." I handed him the original file, then folded my copy. "I'll wait outside."

Trevor didn't keep me waiting. He locked the door behind us, then insisted we walk around to the side door. He used his security pass to gain us entrance to a stairwell. Just as easily, he opened the laboratory adjacent to Damon's office.

"You're a handy guy to have around, Trevor." I walked in and turned on the lights. The arrangement of the room hadn't changed since my days. The big rectangle was set up with ten large lab stations: black tops on stainless steel bases. One long wall was a bank of windows. Under the windows were cabinets, all closed and neatly labeled. The opposite wall held several whiteboards, still filled with lessons and formulas in Damon's handwriting. One narrow end had a door to his office and a set of shelves. The opposite had a refrigerator, sterilization equipment, and the like. The three walls without windows were decorated with colorful shadow boxes, each featuring an element of the periodic table.

"What are we looking for?" Trevor asked as we took it all in.

"Clues," I said, kidding but not. "Look for another computer. Anything that would tell us what he's working on. Oh, and ravens. Look for ravens."

"Ravens," Trevor repeated as he began to explore the outer rim of the room. "Why do you want to know what he was working on now? I thought this was connected to something from the past."

"True, but we don't know that they aren't one and the same."

The search turned over no new leaves. The laptop I'd copied

was the only one here. There were no ravens or anything personal in the working space. I glanced at the man I knew as a boy. "You look good, Trevor. You finally fill that uniform out."

He laughed without looking my way. "My wife is a good cook. We have three kids with the fourth coming in another month." There was pride in his voice.

"Looks like life's been good to you, *Lieutenant* Hargrove. You thought I didn't notice, right? Why is your office still here in the way-back? I would have thought the promotion came with a real office."

"It did. Got a real nice office with a glossy desk and a parking spot with my name on it. Problem is, everyone knows where it is. I come here when I need to get away from interruptions. Don't usually work the night shift either but had a man call off tonight." He stopped searching and faced me. "I think Damon loves her. Hanna. He's never said so, but I got the feeling he's been thinking about marriage. Damon sometimes talked about how they could merge their lives. Hanna becoming a U.S. citizen. Him changing jobs, following her to give her career a chance to get started."

"I saw a picture of them. The look on their faces wasn't something you could fake."

"Assume he is hiding. I don't think he would leave her if he didn't think he was coming back. I don't think he would put her through the strain of disappearing if he had a choice."

"Aren't you just adding weight to the idea that he isn't hiding?"

"Possibly, but..." He blew out a long breath. "This is confidential. God, I hope I'm doing the right thing. The morning before Damon left, he called and asked to use the annex for a meeting. I said sure and then forgot about it. I came over in the afternoon to get something and walked in on the meeting. I apologized, and Damon was quick to accept but the other guy was pissed. He was military. A colonel named Powers."

"Do you know what branch?"

"Army. I'm not supposed to know anything. But they were

arguing. Powers said everything was arranged and there was no changing plans now. Damon said he wasn't going to leave. Powers said it was his choice, his funeral."

Damon Marten was up to his eyeballs in some nasty shit. I had to get to the bottom fast. If the wrong guys had him, then his time was running out.

"I'll figure this out, Trevor. You can trust me. But you can't trust anyone else. Someone else was here tonight, mercenaries looking for something Damon left behind. Don't try to stop them."

"This is my—"

"They'll kill you without a thought and still go after the booty. I sent my husband to work, off to a conference where the biggest danger should have been the airplane food. I got a call twenty-four hours later and flew halfway around the world to bring his body back. It's been over a year, and I still haven't figured out how to live without him. If you love your wife, if you love your kids, don't try to stop these people. Whatever trouble Damon is in, it's not worth your life."

He ran his hands through his hair, fighting warring feelings. And then he looked at me, his eyes large and understanding. "But you're going after him."

"It's what I do."

He looked away, shaking his head. "What about your life?"

My phone rang. Ian. I held up a finger in the international sign for *shut up*. "Yeah."

"Someone broke into Hanna Lang's house. Get your ass there now. Address coming your way."

I headed to the door, Trevor following me. "Someone just broke into Hanna's house."

"She lives with Damon." He stood, sliding his hat back on. "Come on, we'll get there faster with lights and siren." He stepped around me, stopping when I grabbed his arm.

"You can't. You don't know who's watching. I was serious about not wanting you dead. I won't make your wife a widow.

Stay here, do your job, live a good, long life."

Hands on hips, he bit his lower lip as he ran through options. Some things never change. I knew the moment he saw things my way. "Fuck me."

"It's not your fight."

"And it's yours?" The question was cold, an accusation.

"I specialize in lost causes. This is what I do, who I am." I smiled, showing the real me. "Don't worry about me, worry about the other guy. I'm in the mood to kick some ass."

He snorted. "The more things change...fine, we'll play your way but on two conditions. One, you keep me updated."

"I can do that. And two?"

"Don't spill blood on my campus." He smirked. "It's a bitch to get out. Go find Damon and bring him home."

I stepped into the night. Hurrying to my car, I pulled a Superman, stripping off the wig and accessories to reveal my true identity. My extraordinary sense of balance and dexterity had me behind the wheel in record time. Then it was the work of programming the GPS—open the app, and we're loading, loading, loading, and find 3214 Sycamore Crossing. Stupid name. Trees can't cross. And we're mapping, mapping, mapping—then it was the work of seven minutes until I pulled in front of a three-story townhouse.

Small stone courtyards terraced down the sloping street. I walked through the ornamental gate of the one matching the number Ian gave me. The front door opened. Dixon's lanky body briefly filled the lighted space before he joined me in the night. "She's crazy, Diamond. I don't do crazy ladies. Can I have the car keys and I'll meet you at home?"

"You don't have your license, and that car isn't completely street legal. I'm not spending the night pulling you out of jail. Besides, it can't be that bad." I walked past him and pushed the door open.

"Who would do this? Who? Who?" The sound drifted down from above. It wasn't an owl but a different kind of bird. Gasping breaths broke up the words, remnants of a hard jag.

"Damn, Diamond, that didn't come from a fist." Dix touched my cheek, prodding with what felt like a hot poker. "What did this?"

I had to think. "A bicycle. Where are we going?"

"Up," he said, retaking the lead. A staircase at the back of the room took us to the main living floor. Two steps in and I knew the job was professional. The perps went for maximum damage. This wasn't about searching; this was about intimidation. Hanna Lang sat in the corner of the couch on the only cushion. The other two were near her feet, sliced like a body on a coroner's table. Ian sat on the arm of the couch, doing the "poor baby" routine. Hanna's head rested on his thigh. Her hair was wet; she wore pajamas.

"Ian," I said, getting his attention and, by default, hers. "Hanna, are you hurt?"

Ian turned to me and did a double take. His eyebrows asked a question that would have to wait for an answer. Anything I would have said was cut off by our hostess.

"Hurt? Look around. Yes, I'm hurt." She didn't sound hurt; she sounded pissed. "All of our things, destroyed. Is this proof enough for you? Damon didn't walk away to s-screw some b-bitch on a beach. He's been kidnapped."

"I'm going to take a look around." I did. Literally. The open floor plan had spaces rather than rooms, and nearly everything was visible from where I stood. The living room ran the full width of the townhouse and was decorated in tasteful professor. White bookshelves lined the walls, the spaces filled with books, stacks of magazines, glass and ceramic art, and pictures. The area where Hanna sat had a coordinated arrangement of a couch and three chairs, designed for conversation. The remaining third was built for lounging, with or without a book. Every upholstered surface was slashed, stuffing pushing through the gap like it was Thanksgiving Day. A destructive hand had gone after shelves, pulling, flipping, and tossing the bric-a-brac across the carpeting.

The kitchen drawers were open. The refrigerator door gaped wide, contents broken and splattered across the tile part of the floor. The dining room beyond had nothing to take out of place, so the perp had a message carved into the wood in messy, block letters.

GIVE IT TO US AND YOU WON'T GET HURT.

"What is 'it'?" Dixon whispered.

"Working on it," I whispered back. "Upstairs."

The top of the stairs opened into a small landing sporting four doors and one of those crazy narrow tables over which an oil painting of a raven hung. Two smaller rooms to the rear of the townhouse were his-and-hers offices. We started in "his."

"Take the computer," I said, stating the obvious. While Dix got busy with the 0s and 1s, I searched the shelving and tabletops. Damon had a decent amount of geek décor. There were three different models of molecules: alcohol, caffeine, and sugar. He had a collection of what looked like letter blocks children play with. His had the elements of the periodic table. He had arranged some of them into words.

GeNiUS. The braggart.

FArTs. Totally a guy thing.

NeVEr AgAlN "Never again what? Come on, Damon. Talk to me."

I paged through documents. His genius lack of organization made it difficult to discern what he was currently working on. If two of his former colleagues had reached out, I expected he would have resurrected something of the past. Every surface item related to Calvert College.

The closet had fall and winter jackets hanging from the single rod. The shelf above had boxes with years written in thick black marker. A future time killer. On the floor were two duffle bags. I opened the right one. It was filled with neatly folded clothes. His. The left one had hers.

On the end table, next to his couch, was a stack of the latest issues of *Chemistry Research Journal*. In between two editions was a small collection of papers. I recognized a few; they were the articles I'd copied from Trevor's file. Beneath was a poorly torn sheet of legal paper with two names and contact information.

"What's wrong?" Dixon asked.

"Why do you think something is wrong?"

"You're growling."

If I was, it was because, with two people dead, the brilliant Damon Marten left the location of two others where anyone snooping around could find them. Why didn't he just paint bullseyes on their backs? "Just annoyed. You got anything?"

"I'm imaging the hard drive now."

And people say Millennials don't take initiative. "Good work. Go next door and look for Hanna's. She's got secrets we need to know."

"On it," he said, leaving the room.

The intruders hadn't gotten to this floor, but that didn't mean the next ones wouldn't. Damon's computer was coming with us, even though Dixon already owned the files. The collection of notes and contacts was tucked into one of the journals and coming with me.

I went into Hanna's office and found Dixon coaxing the computer to do his bidding. Her taste in décor was feminine without being girly. Prints of wildflowers and a German countryside. Throw pillows on her couch. Decorative lamps. The only geek décor in here had to have been a gift. A picture frame showed her and Damon at the ocean. The bottom of the frame had the periodic elements spelling I Lv U.

It made me smile.

Hanna was studying psychology. Her graduate-level studies, according to the freehand notes, focused on the long-term effects of traumatic events in childhood. She postulated that the adult-child could be unable to assume a productive role in society; could be unable to form mature, adult relationships; and could have the trauma re-manifest as abusive or subversive behaviors but that these characteristics were reversible with interventions.

I glanced between the cursive prognostications of a clinician and the adult-child humming as he illicitly copied a private person's computer at my direction.

I'd have to keep Hanna away from Dixon.

"We're taking Damon's computer with us. When you're done, pack it up along with any other tech you find. I'm going to check out the rest of the floor."

"'K. Are we taking this one, too?"

I weighed the odds of her having information related to Damon's work. Low. That meant I didn't care if Trixie and her Cleaning Ladies or any other fortune hunter out there got it. "No. We'll warn her it's at risk, but it's on her to protect her shit. Be back in a minute."

In the hallway, I looked through the open door at a full bath for a guest. It was perfectly staged, from the unused bar of soap to the attractive accent pieces, all without a hair out of place.

The master bedroom, conversely, had everything out of place, by choice. The bed wasn't made. Hanna's clothes from the day were tossed on a chair. The bathroom was steamy, the shower stall still wet from use. It was the lived-in mess of real people in their real space. A cursory review of the nightstands found romance novels on her side and a mix of horror and thrillers on his.

I returned to the offices, finding Dixon packing Damon's computer. "Take it down to the ground floor. Don't let her see it. Search the garage and those other rooms while you're at it. Maybe we'll get lucky."

"By myself?" he asked quickly, a mixture of anticipation and uncertainty in his voice. "I'll see what the trashers did there. See if I can tell if anything was taken. And if there's anything that should have been taken."

"Right. Include the car in the search. People treat their cars like their second homes or offices. Walk downstairs with me.

When I peel off to talk to Hanna, you just keep on going."

"Do you want me to come get you if I find something?"

"Text me, and I'll make an excuse." We walked down the stairs. I began talking as soon as I could see Hanna, making sure her attention was on me. "You didn't call the police about the break-in? Why weren't they your first call?"

"What were they going to do? Write a report?" Her attitude bitch-slapped my perfectly reasonable question. "We all know this isn't a random crime. Did you see my dining room table?"

I nodded. "What is 'it'?"

"I don't know." For me, she said each word separately. When she looked up at Ian, her lower lip jutted out. "I really don't."

He petted her hair like a cat. "Did Damon have something he prized above other things? Something he was proud of, or possessive of?"

"He just isn't that kind of man. He prized his work but would give it away if someone could use it to build upon, to make it better." Hanna focused on Ian, her champion, never noticing Dixon continuing down the stairs. "For Damon, it really was about protecting people. Soldiers specifically, but more all people."

"Somebody thinks he had something. They weren't subtle about looking for it." Damon had been tipped off by Klemer and Hass, and he took it seriously enough to pack the bags. "Were you and Damon planning to take a trip? Leave town for a few days?"

She shook her head. "The term just ended, but he is teaching a summer class and he is at a critical point in his work. We talked about a long weekend maybe, but not until August."

Not helpful. None of this was helpful. "Walk us through what you did from the time you left my building."

"After our meeting, if you could call it that," she said, her attitude back in place, "I came back here. I parked in the garage and then set the alarm for the night. I went up to my office, got on my computer to look for a *real* professional to help me. I had sent an email to O'Rourke and had decided to give him twenty-four hours before I did try to call your Army. I was tired but knew I'd never sleep, so I took a long shower, trying to figure out what to do next. After my shower, I came downstairs for a glass of wine. That's when I found this." She waved her hand to the room surrounding us. "I knew it wasn't a random break-in. I had put Ian's card down by my phone and called him for help."

"You weren't afraid they were still in the house?"

"I was terrified. I had a moment where I was frozen. My mind, it was going, going, going. Was someone in my house? Why didn't the alarm go off? I ran halfway up the stairs before thinking that maybe that was where they were. I ran back down, into the bathroom and locked the door. Then I called Ian."

I felt like a CGI character dropped in the middle of a long-running game. I didn't know the rules, the territory, or backstory. All I had was the mission. But my interest was piqued, my curiosity awakened. "I'll take the job. Your ten grand will buy you two weeks. Expenses are extra."

She stared, her jaw clenched tight. The little muscle in the corner working hard. "I don't want you. I don't care what O'Rourke said, you are a mean, self-important, arrogant bitch. I wouldn't hire you if you were the last whatever-you-are on the planet!"

"What I am is good at this. Sleep on it if you want, but consider doing it somewhere else. If one person thinks 'it' is in the house, chances are others will too. Ian? You coming?"

"I have to work tonight." He stood, pulling away from the hand that held him. "She really is top in her field. At least take her advice and stay with a friend."

She rose slowly, retracting her claws to become the classic damsel in distress. "Wait...you can't go. How can you be so hard?"

"I'm Diamond. The name says it all." I waved my fingers, ta-ta-ing in her general direction.

Hanna landed in front of me, grabbing my hand and shaking

it. "You're hired. Now you can stay here tonight. You can sleep on the couch or there's a spare bedroom downstairs. I'll make my famous strawberry lemonade spritzers." She stepped back, restoring our personal spaces, looking like the cat that just got a big, fat, bacon-stuffed canary.

I snorted. "Not happening." I had work to do, a mountain of it to turn all these leads into a direction pointing to Damon. I wasn't putting it off to have some pillow-fighting, panty-laden girl party.

"...But..." And then those blue eyes were swimming. The spritzer punch replaced with a don't-leave-me vibrato. "What am I to do?"

Ian rubbed his chin as he looked my way. Dixon blinked at me. I couldn't believe I was back here again.

WHAT PART OF CUPCAKES DON'T YOU UNDERSTAND?

I sat on my remaining kitchen chair, soaking in the Tuscan countryside on my calendar. Focusing, I brought up details of the region. The generous hills, the thick, tall grasses, the crazy steep drop-offs along roads. The sting of a dozen wasps jolted me back to my area code. Ian knelt on my floor attending to a scratch I hadn't felt until he bathed it in firewater. It took a few breaths until I could talk again. "Do you think she's bipolar?"

"Who?" he asked, as if the possible list was infinite.

Pulling the ice pack off my cheek, I twisted to look down at him. "Dixon's new roommate. You remember, the blonde you stroked like a cat."

"Hanna? Why do you think she's bipolar?" His brows were pressed together, his jaw clenched. His hands might have been gentle, but his face read irritated, annoyed.

"You didn't notice? One minute, she's all like, 'Bitch, back off or I'm gonna cut you,' and the next she's batting those big doe eyes, pulling a 'I need a hero, how about you, big boy?'"

"I don't think bipolar is a minute-to-minute kinda swing."

"Are you sure?"

His eyes met mine. "Are you bipolar?"

"No. Of course not." Stupid question.

"Then I'm sure." He went back to work, his hands light on

my battered body. "She's had the rug pulled out from under her. One day, her man is there. The next, he isn't. It messes a person up." He used his teeth to open a bandage wrapper, then applied it. "If anyone got that, I'da thought it would be you. I don't like the look of this one. Probably could have used a stitch or two. Maybe we should run over to Brunhilda's?"

I couldn't feel whatever he was studying on my jawline. And if I couldn't feel it, it definitely wasn't worth a trip to the vet tech who dabbled in humans. "It'll be fine. Are you done?"

"Not even close. Have you looked at yourself? Let me see your arm." He straightened out my right arm, positioning it for access to the soft underside and the five-inch patch of dried blood. "I'm not going to ask what made this."

I leaned back, relaxing until lightning stung my arm, snapping me to attention. "Hate that shit you're using."

"It's good for you. If you think Hanna's playing us, why'd you take the job?"

"I'm curious, I guess. I don't think she's playing us, not exactly. She and Damon are a thing. No doubt. Her man ghosted two days ago and, unlike my sitch, she has a chance of getting hers back. But my trouble sensor is going off, and you know it's never wrong. Irish is up to something, probably the Cleaning Ladies too. I need to catch up. Fast."

He went back to the task at hand. "How did Trixie do this much damage?"

"She didn't do all of it. Fire escapes should be used more than once a decade."

"What did you say did this? It's a weird shape."

I put the ice back in place, covering the shape. "Tortoiseshell." Like I said, anything can be a weapon in the right hands. "She called me slow, Ian. Trixie the Cleaning Lady sounded disappointed to fight me when I wasn't in shape."

"You were slow if she did this much damage." He was matter-of-fact, as though he weren't gutting me. "You've been out of the game for what? Three years? How much weight have you lost?

Thirty pounds? Even eating with a teenage boy, I bet I can see your ribs." He tugged up the hem of my shirt.

I caught his hands, and we locked on each other.

The back door opened, and the aforementioned teenage boy entered, bag of cookies and a sleeping bag. "Hanna's in my room, just like you said. What's next?"

A half hour before noon and the street outside the renovated, historic building in Richmond, Virginia was filled with people to-ing and fro-ing. Men hurried along, suit jackets swishing open and closed with each step. Soon it would be too hot to wear a jacket midday. Women were about the same, although clothing ranged from killer dresses to modest dresses to the feminized version of the classic suit. The phones pressed to their heads were a unisex accessory.

"Jeremy Hardy is a senior scientist at HMB Pharmaceuticals. Um," Dixon paused and when he spoke again, it was with a Cockney accent. "'E worked dere fa tree years."

"What are you eating?"

Pause. "Pop-Tart. We need more."

"I just bought the box."

"Like on Monday. Today's Friday. We need milk, too."

"I should just buy a fucking cow."

"That would be crazy." Pause. "Can we?"

"Tell me how Jeremy Hardy connects to Damon Marten. Why was his name on that sheet of paper in Damon's office?"

"Ian figured that out. They were in the same graduate chemistry program in Germany. All of them were there. Marten, Hardy, the two dead ones, and the other woman, China Whiting. They wrote a few papers together. I emailed them to you."

"What were the papers on?"

"I have no idea. But I can read you the title. The first one is"—he began reading like a kindergartener, one word at a time—"*The Effects of Neurochemical Disrupters on the Alpha*

Receptors in Bovines." He paused. "No idea what it means."

"They tested drugs on cows."

"Really? Why don't they just say that? Do you want the others?"

I listened as he read two more titles themed on the use of antipsychotic drugs to suppress brain activity. I'd have to read the articles to tell you what they were going for. Or ask our friend Jeremy Hardy. I opened the email, reading what fit on my phone. Birthdate. Birth city. Universities and degrees. Blah, blah, blah. "Anything else?"

"I did the research on Hanna. Her mom died when she was like twelve. Same age when my mom took off."

I paused in my reading not because of Hanna but because of Dixon. He had never mentioned his mother before.

"Jeremy lives on the internet," he said, changing the subject.

"Yeah, I studied him last night." I opened my camera roll and the pictures I'd downloaded. I knew his hazel eyes, the professional cut of his sandy brown hair, the scar near the corner of his mouth.

I left the rental car, dressed to blend into the professional crowd but simply enough to move if I had to. Timing was a matter of strategy. I called earlier and confirmed that Jeremy was in his office today. I timed my arrival, posing as the sister of his college roommate, dropping by just in time for an impromptu lunch. I was in town for a few days and saw he worked nearby, etcetera. I knew enough about his roommate to get by, and the few years of difference in our ages wouldn't be enough for Jeremy to question my story.

As I threaded through two cars parked on the opposite side of the road, my quarry came out of the building. He was talking to a man, both were smiling, joking. At the sidewalk, Jeremy went right, his associate left.

And my plan changed.

I followed, lengthening my stride to match his. Jeremy was a man with a destination in mind. This was no casual walk down the block for a sandwich. He checked his watch three times. Around the corner. Cross the street. Around another corner. Two storefronts later, he walked into a restaurant.

New plan. I'd have lunch while Jeremy does the same. When he's done, he'd be reacquainted with the former roommate's sister who recognized him across the restaurant. Ain't life a coincidence?

I knelt to tie a shoe that didn't need tying, then rose and studied my phone, creating working space between me and my quarry. I put a smile on my face and entered the restaurant like I belonged there. Which I did. I looked around, hoping to spot Jeremy to inform my next move. He was at the bar, just to my right. Two bartenders in the usual uniform worked the large U-shaped bar. Four booths lined the front windows, another five covered the far wall. More than half were seated.

"Natasha?" Jeremy Hardy's expression was open, friendly, and hopeful.

And my plan changed. Again.

Yeah, I could be Natasha.

Whoever she was.

"Jeremy?" I transformed my face to mirror his.

"I knew it was you. The way you walked in, like you commanded the room, I said, there's a woman who could run a chain of bakeries without getting flour on her face."

Chain of bakeries. Got it.

"We can get a table. Unless you rather stay in the bar?"

The bar had a door marked "Emergency" that opened directly to the street. This gave me two means of egress. "Let's stay in here. The booths along the wall look...inviting." What they were was dark and private. The perfect place for questioning a witness.

Jeremy's smile broadened. "Let me just tell the bartender." He took care of business while I claimed the last booth in the row. It would ensure he focused on me while I had a full view of the room. He joined me at the booth, the bartender arriving coincidently with menus and water. He added iced tea. I did not.

And then we were two strangers, sitting together with nothing between us but thirty inches of white tablecloth.

"Have you done this often?" he asked. "Had lunch?"

The question could not be as pedestrian as it sounded. In the playbook of life, there is a go-to drill when you are in a conversation and have no idea what's going on.

"'Often' might be too strong of a word. You?" Some might call it a volley, always putting the ball back in the other court.

"A few times. I wasn't sure I would like it. You know how it is."

Others might call it a quarterback sneak. "Yes, but it's like the famous dead guy said, 'Nothing ventured, nothing gained.'"

"And venture belongs to the adventurous. Like us." He laughed. "That famous dead guy was Navjot Singh Sidhu, and he isn't dead. Also doubt he was talking about this."

I dismissed the counterpoint with a friendly wave of my fingers. "Applies all the same." I call it the alley-oop. It's a foolproof way of carrying on an extended conversation without saying a thing. Politicians do it daily.

"I suppose. All's fair in business and dating."

Dating.

I was on one of those blind lunch date things. Which meant at some point, Natasha the Baker was going to make an appearance.

Elbows on the table, I cupped my chin and gave him my cute grin. "How about we skip the usual stuff? Let's not be ordinary. Tell me the most crazy, unusual thing you've done or an off-the-beaten-path place you've been."

He considered me with a cocked head, a dog processing a new idea.

When nothing came, I seeded the cloud. "I'll start. After college, I went to Italy with a friend. He knew someone, who knew someone, and we ended up staying in a Hungarian convent, complete with nuns. I was new to international travel and, yes, this is my way to say what happened was not my fault. I wouldn't turn over my passport, even to nuns. They tell you to keep it under your control at all times, right? So, I was keeping it. He kept his, put it away in a drawer in the night table. Which is where it stayed when we left four days later for Florence. Still say…not my fault."

He laughed, leaning into the table, engaged. "I did a post-grad stint in Germany."

God, I love when witnesses cooperate.

"I was on a research grant, experimenting with a new class of drugs that showed promise for chronic pain management. It was strictly *verboten* from experimenting on ourselves. But I was in my twenties and immortal and—God, I can't believe I'm admitting this."

"You dosed yourself."

His eyes sparkled with mischief. "Suffice it to say that I ended up with two broken thumbs."

I chuckled, understanding the attraction, the curiosity, the dumbassedness. "Were you alone? I can tell there's more to the story. You had 'friends' with you who did it too, right?"

"Busted. There were five of us. Knoll broke his nose and looked like a raccoon for a week. Damon messed up his shoulder and had to learn to write left-handed. The other two, Monica and China, were pissed that we did it." He laughed at his younger self. "This is a lot more interesting than the usual 'Do you like your job?' and 'How did you get where you are?'"

"Agree. And you have got me curious…did your work get to market?"

His smile faded, retreating until even his gaze was down. "The work, uh, went a different direction. I didn't agree and left."

"Aw, I'm sorry. What happened?"

"Two of the others, Monica and Damon, they were more interested in military applications than humanitarian ones. Knoll was trying to get into Monica's pants and would agree if she said the sky was green. China always went with the crowd."

"It's rough when you discover you were someone's friend, but they weren't yours. I can't tell you the number of times I tripped over 'friends' when I was starting my business. Empty promises. Missed deadlines. Half-assed quality. There were a few years when I wouldn't work with anyone I knew socially. It wasn't worth it."

A woman stepped into the bar. She had dark hair and looked around anxiously. She carried a cake box.

Jeremy's cell rang. "I'm sorry. I need to take this. It's Carly, my admin. She wouldn't call unless it was an emergency."

"Not a problem. I'll just sneak away to the ladies' room." I slid out of the booth as he answered the call. The real Natasha had retreated to the foyer, standing in the window to see the people approaching. I needed her on the other side of that glass. "Excuse me? Natasha?"

She turned and, no, she didn't look a thing like me. "Yes?"

"Hi, I'm Jeremy's admin, Carly. We had an emergency come up and he was dispatched to one of our facilities." I leaned in, glanced left, then right. "An experimental gas for the delivery of growth hormones went awry, and apparently the men are spontaneously sprouting breasts."

She gasped. "No."

I nodded solemnly. "Big ones. Forty-two, triple D."

"Damn." She glanced to her own well-supported set. "I understand. I, uh, I made these for him. Maybe you could put them on his desk?"

"Aww, you're so sweet. I promise, I'll make sure he calls you." I crossed my heart.

"Thank you. Breasts, huh?" She left, still shaking her head.

I peeked in the box. Four cupcakes sat in a cardboard cutout, smelling like spun sugar. I stopped at the first table. "Excuse me," I said to the four men. "My almost-boyfriend's mother gave me these cupcakes as a birthday gift, but I can't eat them because I'm borderline alcoholic. I can't throw them away. Too much guilt. Could you please take them?" I opened the box. The cupcakes sold themselves.

The booths remaining had filled up. A motley cast for a

posh, professional neighborhood.

"I'm just glad you're not hurt," Jeremy said as I approached the table. "No, of course I don't. Take the rest of the day off." He waved me into my seat. "It doesn't make sense. Try to put it out of your mind." He took another minute to soothe, cajole, before the call ended. "The world is a crazy place," he said to me.

"Sounds serious. What happened?"

"Carly was attacked in our parking garage."

I was on alert now, not liking the timing. "Oh, no. Is she hurt?"

"Bruised, it sounds like. More scared than anything. The really bizarre thing was, they didn't want her purse or her money, just her phone."

"That is weird."

"She was taking an early lunch to go to a doctor's appointment, talking on her phone while she went to the parking garage. It's at the end of the block. It's safe. Nothing like this has happened before. Someone body-slammed her into an SUV. They asked her a few times who she worked for, where I was. They shoved her to the ground, took her phone, then ran. Someone found her, called the police."

"Did they take her to the hospital?"

"She refused to go. Went back to the office, and the police were called. It wasn't random. Corporate espionage springs to mind but, my God, attacking my admin? She's twenty-six and has to weigh a hundred twenty pounds. Plant a spy, seduce my team, but don't get heavy-handed with a young woman."

"Are you working on something that valuable?" My gut said this was connected to Damon, but my gut didn't know the whole story. Maybe Jeremy was cracking the code to change water to wine.

"The company is, sure, but not me. I'm not in the research division. What I know could compromise our competitive edge, but it's just business." He became quiet, introspective. The attack on his assistant was outside his norm. His expressive face showed the consideration and rejection of ideas.

A head poked out of a booth in front of us. An ugly head. The nose must have been broken six or seven times. He stepped into the narrow strip of land between the booths and the barstools. Ugly was skinny, his jacket hanging as though his shoulders were a wire hanger. I could take him. Trixie had more meat on her than this guy.

Jeremy twisted around, following my gaze. "Is something wrong?"

"Things are about to get interesting."

A guy with a toothpick hanging between his lips fell in behind Ugly. Close to three hundred pounds balanced on thick pins he called legs. Brute force wasn't going to work for me with this guy. I doubted he'd notice if I landed a punch to his prominent paunch.

Suddenly the secluded corner was a trap with no room to work. Needing out, I lifted the phone to my ear and spoke loudly. "Dad? Are you there? I can't hear. Hold on, let me get to a quieter spot." I spoke aside to a confused Jeremy. "I'll be right back. Just stay where you are. When I say move, you do it like your ass is on fire." I slipped out of the booth. "Okay, I'm here. What did Digger do?" I deliberately bumped into Ugly. "Sorry." Not sorry. Answer to question one: yes, there was hardware packed under that jacket. Toothpick wasn't packing. His shirt stretched over his body like a condom over a bowling ball. No secrets there. "He didn't. That ass. I can be there in an hour. I just need to take care of something."

Now on the flipside of our company, I tucked my phone into an inside pocket and interrupted the senior citizens at the last booth before the door to the street. "Mind if I borrow this?" Without waiting for permission, I took the medical cane with its squat little legs, twirling it to get a sense of the weight.

I'd used worse.

"Young lady?" the elder voice called to my back. "Young lady, bring that back this instant."

Toothpick twisted his thick torso, hearing or sensing trouble.

Lunging the last step, I swept the cane up, taking out Toothpick's knees. The ponytail that neatly contained five inches of thick hair was the handhold I yanked. I put a little wrist into it—and a lot of shoulder—sending Toothpick into the lineup of barstools.

Strike!

The stools fell among shouts and a few unladylike utterances. Arms and legs, purses, and furniture had Toothpick out of the fray.

Ugly turned around. "What the—" A cane to the vocal cords curtailed the rest of it. An upward swing followed, catching him under the chin. He staggered backward past Jeremy and into the alcove for the waitstaff.

I followed Ugly, issuing an order. "Now, Jeremy. Get to the door." I swung the cane. Ugly caught it, grinning like a jack-o-lantern. My fist broke his nose for the eighth time. His hands went to his face. I reclaimed the cane and swept his legs out. He rode the wall down, meeting the floor with a sharp smack and a flurry of curses.

That kind of language, and in a public place.

Some people have no manners.

Jeremy skirted past Toothpick, still stuck on his back, one leg tangled up in a barstool. The civilians were disentangling. Confused, looking as though a hurricane had snuck up on them, they weren't helping Toothpick. Yet.

I leapt over the mess, took Jeremy's arm, and ushered him to the emergency exit. I paused long enough to return the cane to its original, upright position. "Thank you for your support. This concludes the entertainment portion of our show."

"The hell it does," the owner said, palms on the table to push himself up. His wife put her hand on his elbow, holding him back.

"Smart woman. Lunch is on me." I tossed a few bills on the table. "Jeremy, let's go." I pushed him toward the door.

"That says emergency exit only." He wasn't stupid. The sudden eruption of violence was a shock to his well-ordered world.

I shoved him out. "Do you have a minimum on how much blood has to be spilled for it to be an emergency?"

Out in the sunlight and open sidewalk, I headed him back toward my car. He was less than cooperative. "I just—can you stop?" He did. "What happened back there, Natasha?"

"No stopping." I wrapped my arm around his and got him moving. "Whoever attacked your assistant was looking for you."

"Me?" He stopped again.

"No. Stopping." And we were moving again. I scanned the street, searching for new threats. The street was lined with parked cars. Silhouettes in the driver's seat made every vehicle look like a target. "The project you worked on in Germany. Someone wants it."

"I don't understand. Listen, Natasha—"

"Diamond. I'm here to save your ass. Knoll and Monica are dead."

"No." The fucker stopped. Again.

"Yes. Damon is missing. Now someone has found you, and you're making it easy for them, standing on the sidewalk like a goddamn statue." I wrapped his tie around my hand and used it as a leash. We rounded the corner. This was a security nightmare. We couldn't have been more exposed if we were butt naked on a beach. "We need to get out of the open."

He slowed, despite the pressure on his neck, and pointed over his shoulder. "Is that car coming at us?"

Broad daylight, middle of downtown Richmond, a minivan barreled out of a turn too wide to stay on the road.

I didn't have to tell Jeremy to run. A burn stung as his tie ripped out of my hand. I took off after him. Pedestrians were walking toward us. "Out of the way. Move!" I dared a glance over my shoulder. Two tires on the sidewalk, two on the road, the van was closing in. Fire hydrants and power poles and trees were immovable obstacles protecting our asses. "Across," I yelled. "Don't stop."

At the corner, Jeremy didn't hesitate, running into the road.

Horns blared as drivers on the busier main street accommodated us. "The alley," he shouted. "I know a shortcut."

I followed him into the lane too narrow for a delivery truck. Horns roared again. The minivan hadn't hesitated any more than we did. Traffic split like the Red Sea, directing the deadly fucker to us. "That wasn't supposed to happen. Faster!"

"I don't have a faster."

I didn't either. "It's faster or dead. Your choice."

We kicked into high gear, the minivan now in the narrow alley.

"He can't do that. This is a one-way street." Jeremy shouted each word, outraged. He pulled ahead of me.

We were sandwiched between two brick buildings. Man doors and overhead doors dotted the corridor, but all were closed. I tried a few, as much as I could. Nothing opened. Straight was our only option.

A box truck turned into the alley. So, I was wrong. The truck did fit with about a foot to spare on either side.

A metal door covered in graffiti rolled open quickly. A man stood under the door, the arms that pushed it up still extended. A forklift waited just inside. The man stepped into the alley, waving the truck in, oblivious to the forty-five-hundred pounds of blunt force trauma coming at him.

"Get back!" I yelled.

Why is it when you need people to move their fastest, they go glacier?

"Inside!" I ordered. Jeremy complied, diving to his right. It wasn't graceful, but it got him out of the line of fire. Glacier-man stood, blinking. Brakes locked; tires squealed. I lunged at the man, tackling him through the open door and onto the forklift.

The maniac van driver lost control, swerving dangerously. Brick wall. Brick wall. Bollard. Metal and fiberglass and plastic screamed as the four-foot-high yellow, concrete post put an end to the chase.

I pushed at his shoulders, unburying the stranger's face from my chest. Not a first but usually involved alcohol and personal regrets. This time, my only regret was the edge of the flat fork across my shoulder blade. "Everyone good?"

"Gawd. He could have killed us." A hand went to my stomach, a knee between my legs.

Jeremy helped him to his feet, then did the same for me. "He would have killed us if you hadn't opened the door."

Panting like a dog, I planted my hands on my legs and sucked wind. Instantly, Trixie's voice was in my head. *You've lost your moves. You're as dull as peanut butter.*

Bitch!

Head up, shoulders back, not even close to breathing like a smoker, I went to the minivan. The airbag hadn't gone off. The driver was out. I pressed my fingers to his neck to distinguish between out cold and checked out.

His pulse was there, steady and strong.

"Jeremy, see if this thing still drives." I opened the back door. Before I could stuff the unconscious body in, I had to move the child's car seat, the toys, laundry, God knew what else.

Wait, no I didn't.

"Shouldn't we call the police?" our personal savior asked. "Or at least an ambulance?"

"We'll handle it. We're professionals." I pushed the driver back and undid the seat belt. His one hundred seventy pounds went onto my shoulder, then onto the crap in his back seat. If you think you saw my knees nearly buckle, you should make an appointment with your optometrist.

"What do you do?" he asked Jeremy.

"I sell pharmaceuticals. Professionally. And legally."

"Jeremy," I said. Chitchat could only get us in trouble. "We have to go. Thanks for saving our lives."

Our hero came back into the alley. "Same goes. I'll guide you out. Least I can do."

Jeremy put the van in gear. It took a little gas to separate the van from concrete. Part of the grill opted to stay behind. "I can't believe that all really happened." With the miracle of the backup camera, he eased out of the alley to the main street. "When we get back to my office—"

"You don't understand the situation. Driver here, Ugly, and Toothpick were looking for you, hunting you. Think of them like lions on the Serengeti. You are the lonely gazelle, separated from your pack. The last thing you want to do is go stand in the watering hole. You need to find some cover and get down until the lions are gone."

Driver groaned, coming out of his headbanger sleepy time by millimeters.

"While it's just the two of us," I said to Jeremy, "tell me more about what you all were working on in Germany." He jerked his chin to me, narrowly avoiding a pedestrian flaunting her right-of-way. "Eyes on the road. Now, you were working on a treatment for pain management?"

"That would have been one application. It was promising for Parkinson's as well as Alzheimer's and physical brain injuries. Basically, we found that we could block off parts of the brain that were shorting out, allowing new pathways to be utilized. To use an analogy, we created a chemical 'road closed' barricade. The brain compensated not by stopping but by finding a detour, just like traffic."

"Fascinating. So, you could pinpoint the application of the drug to that extent? Certainly, you couldn't block off entire sections of the brain. That would have caused serious repercussions, cognitive as well as physical."

"We were working on the application part. That was my area of research, and I was making headway. The others were impatient. Computer simulations supported the theory that targeted application would limit the impacted area. Conversely, they indicated that introduction into the blood stream would impact the entirety of the brain, albeit more mildly."

"Acting as a sedative?"

"Not exactly. It didn't induce sleep as much as paralysis."

"People would be awake but frozen?"

"Yes, which was dangerous because if the heart and lungs were to shut down, well..."

"Game over. What was Damon's role?"

"He was the lead chemist, working on the formulary. Knoll was the overall project lead, but without Damon, he had nothing. It was Knoll who first proposed adapting the project from medical research to military. There had been a hostage situation—a paramilitary group had taken over a shopping mall. Sixteen died before it was over. Knoll felt what we were working on could be used to, in simple terms, freeze the situation, allowing authorities to take control without civilian collateral damage. His father worked for the military, he was a colonel in the Air Force, I think. Knoll led, the others followed."

"But not you?"

"I did, for a while. You have to understand, there was so much outrage, so much grief over what had happened in that mall, it seemed a moral obligation to do what we could. I'm pulling over." He found a quiet spot on a little street. "We wanted to see how our compound would perform in a full test. We broke every rule ever written. I don't know who owned the farm. We were in the middle of nowhere, at least, it felt like we were. We set up on the edge of a pasture and had this fan. We misted the serum into the air. It was supposed to drift over the cattle and put them in a state of temporary paralysis. We had calculated the dosage. It should have lasted about fifteen minutes and then worn off." He paused, shaking his head.

"What went wrong?"

He laughed sardonically. "Everything. The wind shifted. We had to run to get out of the way of our own experiment. It drifted over us, into the trees bordering the pasture. There were black birds—someone said they were ravens—they began squawking. They didn't chirp but screamed in sharp, frantic tones. They took to the air. They didn't fly together, in one direction like you're used to seeing. No. It was like, random, scattered. They crashed into each other. They flew into the ground. One by one, they dropped." He swallowed hard; his face twisted as if about to be sick. "They were all dead. Not one survived. We fell apart after that. I came home. As soon as my feet were on the ground, I knew I wasn't going back. They must have known it, too, because they didn't press."

"Knoll and Monica are dead. Damon is missing. Now there's been an attempt on you. Someone wants your work. Who?"

Jeremy wiped the back of his hand across his mouth. "It was so long ago."

Driver moaned now. He inhaled deeply, then opened his eyes. "What?" He lifted a hand, picking up the pink bunny. "Where am I?"

I leaned over him, filling his vision, blocking out Jeremy. "Your messed-up back seat. Stay where you are. Who are you working for? Why did you try to kill us?"

"Kill you? No. I was just supposed to find him. He stole money from a guy who knows a guy I know." Driver was folded into an awkward fetal position, pinned between the seats. He tried to stretch, then subsided when it didn't work.

"You tried to run us down. What the hell was with that if you weren't trying to kill us?"

"Wasn't my fault. You kept running. I had to keep up."

So many questions popped into my head, but none were relevant. There was only one I needed to know. "Who is this 'guy' paying you?"

"I don't know his name." How do they never ask for names? "I just, look, I was just trying to pick up some extra money. My daughter is sick. A buddy asked if I'd help him out with a job. A grand, cash, for a few hours of work. Can I sit up? I really need to."

"Slowly." I hadn't felt a weapon when I moved Driver. "You're going to cooperate, aren't you..."

"Elliot," he said, filling in the blank. "Yeah, I'm going to coopera—shit! What happened to the van?" He leaned between the front row seats, into my space. "My wife's gonna kill me."

"You drove into a concrete post. Gave yourself that nice ornament on your forehead. Ever heard of a seat belt? And why didn't your airbag go off?"

"The airbag? God, I'm glad my kids weren't in the car."

"Way to swing from kidnapper to responsible parent. Now, I want the whole story. Names. Phone numbers. Everything."

Elliot wasn't the fount of information I had hoped. I walked away with names for Ugly and Toothpick and a phone number. According to Elliot, the three hadn't known each other before meeting this morning at a diner. I tended to believe him. He was guileless. In a minivan. As a getaway driver, he was the bottom of the barrel.

This was the downside of a boom economy. Anyone who was any good was already working. What was left, well...

I took a fistful of hair at the back of his head and swung his attention to me. "What your wife can do is a molehill compared to the mountain I'm ready to drop on your ass. Do I have your attention?"

His eyes were blue. We were close enough that I saw every individual striation floating in that sea of white. "Yes, ma'am."

Okay, I liked that.

"You have a choice. One, you work for me." I threw out a number for the privilege of working for me, a retainer so to speak. "Your first assignment is to connect me to your former employer. Soon as they contact you, you'll contact my guy. You don't give anything away about our arrangement, just play along. You agree?"

Elliot pressed the spot soon to be a lump on his head. "What's my other choice?"

I leveled him with a look sharp as a razor blade.

"You gonna kill him?" Jeremy's voice broke. "Would you, would you really do that?"

See what happens when you have a reputation? Everyone thinks your first move is nuclear. I do have other weapons in my arsenal.

"I agree," Elliot answered hastily. "Whatever you want. I wasn't looking for trouble, just some extra money."

I picked up Elliot's cell and held it out. "Unlock it. I'll enter the contact."

He tapped the digits. "Okay. Okay."

I entered Ian's number, the one his customers used. "Your next task will be to make my friend here disappear. My guy will help with resources."

"No. He just tried to kill us. I'm not going anywhere with him." Jeremy had a valid point, but I only had two hands. I needed help. Compare Elliot to Ugly and Toothpick. They were lifers. I'd bet good money this was Elliot's first gig. The man pulling a plastic cow from under his back wasn't hard, he wasn't practiced. He brought a god damn minivan to a kidnapping.

Ian would have to watch him, coach him, but I didn't have a lot of options.

"He's your driver. You have any concerns, you call me." I turned to Elliot. "He calls me and life as you know it is over." Back to Jeremy. "Prove you're as smart as your resume says. Don't call anyone. Don't tell anyone who you are or where you are. Just disappear."

Just like Damon.

"But, I don't want them to worry." Jeremy slowly shook his head, a first step down the path of stupidity.

"Worry or mourn. Pick one. If you listen to me, we'll keep them mutually exclusive." When he still looked undecided, I rolled my eyes. "Look, take the help or don't. It's your funeral. Elliot, take me to the train station, then drop Mr. Conflicted off wherever he wants. I got things to do."

POE SMART GIRL SEEKS BLACK-ASSED RAVEN

My team huddled around a pizza, digesting the information I'd brought back from Richmond along with the pepperoni. I sat at the other end of the table, studying the leaf atop my fork trying to pass itself off as salad. I wasn't slow and I hadn't lost my edge, but speed and sharpness were not honed on pies. That was what I told myself. Over and over. I pretended to be happy eating my nutritiously dense, vitamin-fortified dinner.

It was weeds. Ranch dressing didn't hide it.

"My God," Hanna said, her face pale. "I thought it had something to do with his work now. Not fifteen years ago. His work with the Army is groundbreaking. I could see why every country wanted it."

"Damon didn't talk about what he did in grad school?"

"We didn't talk about work much. We're in different fields, you know? He would try talking to me, but it was just..." She shrugged. "Just noise. When I would talk, his eyes would go blank."

"He didn't talk about Knoll and Monica?"

"Yes, of course he did, but not in specifics. I could see he worried, but he wouldn't talk about it."

This was stupid. I reached for a slice.

Ian pie-blocked me, pretending not to notice my claim. "Did

Damon talk about ravens or a raven? There's a theme here. Damon's obsession with ravens. Ravens on the farm in Germany. Trixie looking for Poe's raven."

Hanna chuckled now, amused. "Poe was one of the things he talked about. A lot." The smile faded then. "But now that I think about it, last week he said something that didn't make sense. He said there are some things in life you can't make up for, no matter how hard you try. He looked at me then, with this intensity, and said he did try. He would do whatever it took. Then he started reciting Edgar Allan Poe's poem 'The Raven.'"

A single slice of pie remained. My mouth watered at the idea of the tang of tomato. It was mine.

Dixon swooped in, stealing my piece and swallowing half of it in a single, Godzilla-like bite. "I made progress on the video. Picked him up in a white Audi."

"Was a woman driving?" Hanna asked, a thin veil of defiance over despair.

"Nope. A man. Now that I know what I'm looking for, I'll be able to track him. It'll take a little time."

Hanna's shoulders sagged with relief. "Could you tell if he was hurt?"

Dix shook his head as he destroyed the last of the pizza. "Was arguing," he said with his mouth full. Then he mimed hands waving in a flurry.

I shoved the salad away. "Ian, I need you to dive deep on the dipshits who I danced with in Richmond."

"And your newest employee. Really? A grand a month retainer? You keep throwing away money like this and you aren't going to have any."

He wasn't wrong.

I didn't care.

"Jeremy go into hiding?"

"Yes. He's on his way to one of my safe houses. Elliot had something to do with that, I think. He's sharp. He got a call from the money people and, with one of Dixon's apps, traced it to Boston. Friend of mine is checking out the location."

"Good. Let me know when we have a name. I'm going to work. Don't bother me unless all hell breaks loose." I left the trio in my home sweet home and went into my office suite. Dixon had done something to my computer and now it moved like it had jet propulsion. I skipped over the background on Hanna, going straight for the goods: Damon's email. Projecting the images on the series of screens referred to as my media room, I focused on his personal email. Seventy-five percent of the current and deleted files were minutia. Daily newsletters, sales, coupons, bait, switches. The folders contained exactly what they claimed to be. Travel. Utilities. Students. I went line by line through folders labeled Chemistry, Friends, and Poe.

I started with Poe. Waste of time. Damon subscribed to a Poe fan club, saving the monthly e-newsletters. In Friends, I found Monica Hass. The email exchange was brief and enigmatic.

Knoll is dead, Monica wrote, *and it wasn't an accident.* She warned him to protect himself. Damon asked for proof, for reason. Her answer:

Someone knows what we did.

Thanks to Jeremy Hardy, I was now a someone.

We destroyed everything, Damon wrote. *There was nothing left.*

That doesn't seem to matter. I'm leaving the country for a while. Be smart and do the same.

Run? From who? Damon's last message was never answered.

Five hours had passed in the blink of an eye. There was nothing more to do with the emails. Not tonight. I stood, stretched, cracked a few joints.

When I graduated, Damon had given me an anthology of Poe's writing. He did it for all his graduate students. Before I set the fire that "killed me," I took the most important things out of the house. Most were treasures Gavriil had given me. Tokens from our time together. A few other items made the cut, including the anthology.

My own little library was the front room of my office. Fifteen feet wide, twenty feet long, the bookshelves lining the walls were only half full. Stacked neatly among textbooks and manuals was my own hard-bound, mass-produced copy, complete with a poorly designed raven on the cover. Passing over the seven-foot-long table, I sank into one of the comfortable chairs and turned on the reading light.

Night settled around me as I opened to page seven fifty-four. I began to read.

*Once upon a midnight dreary, while I pondered…*what was the connection between now and all those years ago? No answer came.

Focus, I ordered, and began again.

*Once upon a midnight dreary, while I pondered…*who was behind its resurrection?

Shifting, I closed my eyes, lifted my chin, and took a deep breath. There was something in this poem. A clue. A reference. My attention would go where I wanted it, not drift to questions I couldn't answer. Three more breaths, deep, long, slow.

I opened my eyes. Then blinked three, four, five times. Where my shelves had been half bare, they now were stacked full of books. Where my walls had been unadorned plaster, there were more shelves, more leather-bound books in a row.

A fire burned low in a fireplace that didn't exist. The heat warmed my face, my hands, my bare feet. Beneath my hands, a heavy book laid on my lap. The pages fell wide, open to "The Raven." The smell of old paper surrounded me.

Something was here. Something I needed to know. I rose, setting the book on my chair. Gone was my vestige of modern-day comfort bought online without trying it out. Here was a winged-back chair in a cream-colored fabric embroidered with ravens, no two of which were the same.

A soft but distinct knock disrupted the silence.

I looked over my shoulder. My door was plain and metal, painted to hide the fact it didn't belong. The door before me was a work of art with twelve carved panels. And, yes, someone was knocking.

I stalked across the room, flinging open the door, anxious for the answer trying to find me.

There was nothing.

I poked my head into the hallway, which looked exactly as it was supposed to. Still nothing.

I closed the door. My fingers traced the relief of the door panels, each a scene from the poem I fell asleep reading.

The knock came again. I opened the door again.

This time, a bird flew in. It flew in a tight circle around the room before landing on the white bust of a man. The face was Sam Irish. I didn't need my subconscious to tell me he was behind this game. I knew that.

The bird on his head watched me. The wings were a woodsy brown, the breast pumpkin orange. A robin.

My arch enemy.

"What the fuck are you doing in a dream about a raven?"

The bird opened its mouth, its voice like the notes from a flute. "Lenore."

"Diamond," I said as I slowly retreated to the fireplace. "Get it right." The man in the poem had a nice little back-and-forth dialog with his subconscious. I preferred action. My fingers curled around the grip of the fireplace poker, the cast iron settling into my palm. "You want to tell me what's hidden in this poem? There's a key here, isn't there, one that opens up this mystery. Just tell me what you know."

The bird stretched its wings, then settled again. The beady little black eyes never left mine. "Nevermore."

"That's the way you want to play? Fine. Don't say I didn't give you a chance." I leapt, aiming for that plump, orange belly. The bird soared overhead, higher than the ceiling should have allowed. "Nevermore," it chirped, taunting, teasing, circling. "Nevermore."

I leapt as I chased it, swinging the iron, looking to skewer the bird. The robin changed directions in an instant, evading my weapon, engorging my irritation. The creature haunted me, both in life and in dreams. I deserved a raven as a spirit animal, or at least a crow. A big, black, noisy crow that stood its ground. I whipped the poker again, getting closer. A feather floated down. Unperturbed, the bird landed on Irish's head and watched.

I prowled closer, closer, the poker behind my back. My voice was soft and coaxing, diametrically opposed to my words. "You are ordinary. Average. Mediocre. You are all the things I am not and refuse to be." I swung the weapon with intent to kill. The poker's claw dug deep into Irish's eye, shattering the bust.

The robin rose above the fray and settled on the remnants of the base. "Nevermore."

The exertion took its toll. My hands ached. My shoulders tired. "I hate you."

"You've lost your moves," the robin said in Trixie's voice. "You're as dull as peanut butter."

A war cry preceded my attack, short-lived as it was. The strike was inches shy and buried the iron in the depths of the plaster wall. But I would not quit. I would not give up. "You're useless. Irrelevant. Pointless." I hurtled words as I did books, the latter striking against plaster a hundred years old with a sound like distant gunfire and again as leather smartly slapped hardwood.

The robin ducked the first book. Deked out the second. Took flight while the third was airborne. I gave chase. "You won't curse me. I am the master of my life. Not you. Never you." The classics flew across the room. Thuds and booms and crashes came. Tomes hit with force enough to bounce back, attacking my position. I leapt and stepped and danced until a foot on a book brought me down.

My heart pounded. My lungs labored. Sprawled on the floor in defeat, I let my head rest on my arm. The cold, metallic taste in my mouth was a testament to what my life had become.

The robin tweeted, this time sounding like a normal robin.

The sound clear and beautiful. I lifted my head, hating it yet unable to ignore it.

"This poem isn't about you," I said breathlessly, my usual bravado gone. "It's not about some mangy raven or Nevermore. It's about a man missing a woman, and her name is Lenore."

I leapt to my feet, back in my own room, back to myself. "Sonofabitch. I have to find Lenore."

HELIUM RHENIUM IODINE AMERICIUM

Lenore was the key. Lenore. The poem, for all of the endless whining about some stupid bird, was actually about a woman. I had the key, now I just needed the lock. I flicked the light on in Dixon's bedroom. "Hanna, wake up."

The gorgeous blonde in the steampunk bed sat up gasping, her hand sliding under her pillow. "What's happened?" She shaded her eyes with her arm. "Damon! Is he..."

"No, but I figured out his clue. It isn't about a damn bird, it's about Lenore."

"The woman in the poem?"

"The woman Poe obsessed about in the poem. I hear Damon was the same with you."

She leveled her eyes at me, her voice flattened in a *I-know-you-aren't-going-there* tone. "He loves me. It's real and mutual and healthy, not an obsession."

"Tomayto, tomahto." I dropped down on the bed, ready for some girl time. "Somewhere in your head is the lock that will open this up."

For fifteen minutes, we explored every avenue of their time together. Hanna was good at it, her psychology background actually having a use. Eventually, we faced the only conclusion we could.

There was nothing in Hanna's head.

I mean, there was a lot of stuff in her head. She was a smart, savvy woman who escaped a tyrannical family to fall in love with an adoring man. But she knew next to nothing about Damon's work or his life prior to their meeting. He hadn't told her any cryptic messages or left any Mensian riddles.

"What do we do now?" Hanna asked the exact question I was chewing on.

"Well, we aren't quitting. If the Cleaning Ladies are looking for this raven thing, that means someone is putting up real cash. Trixie isn't cheap. So, let's assume we aren't looking for a raven, but Lenore. A woman, or something that represents a woman. Anything in your home fit the bill?"

Her eyes darted left and right as she silently walked through the rooms in her house. "Maybe?"

"Alright." Close a door, open a window. End of conversation, time for action.

"You're going to the house, right?" She threw back the covers, shoved her feet into sandals. "I'm coming, too."

I didn't need company, but could Hanna recognize something I would overlook? Maybe. Possibly. "You got ten minutes. Meet me in my office. I need to pack."

Damon was in his second year as a professor at Calvert when I started as a student. He didn't impress me at first. I would have dismissed him as another nerd more comfortable with books than people if he hadn't come to my rescue. Using the spine I didn't know he had, he took a stand in front of the discipline board and accepted responsibility for me from that point on.

I knew then, he was one messed-up man.

Two years later, I became his assistant, a position usually reserved for graduate students. After six years, I knew his habits better than anyone. I had to; it was my job.

People often keep their secrets close for the sense of security, which made his home my first choice. He had bought the townhouse the spring after I started working for him. I had only been there a few times over my college career to check on things when he took vacations or went to conferences.

Standing in her pajamas on the concrete square that was her porch, Hanna unlocked the door. She turned on the light in the foyer, leading the way in. It was small, with only a table for mail and keys. "Where do we start?"

"No place like the present," I said, opening the adjoining door to the garage. "Anything with any reference to a woman, Lenore, or a raven, we want to look at. You've seen everything here a thousand times. Now you need to look through a new lens."

The garage, the car, and the foyer took us minutes. We found golf club head covers shaped like ravens and the small pack Hanna used when biking. They were what they were and nothing more.

Hanna proved to be a good partner. She was methodical, thoughtful, without all the chatter some are prone to. She went through the main floor almost dispassionately, pausing only over a picture of the two of them.

Over the course of two hours, we took the place down to toothpicks. From bottom to top, we searched for false drawers, wall safes, hidden compartments. We thoroughly explored cold air returns, ceiling panels, cabinets. We would have looked under the floorboards, except they were vinyl. If it moved, we tipped it, spun it, took it apart.

Our booty? Five dollars and thirty-two cents, nine university pens, one flash drive (keeper), six socks (no pairs), and one bra. I opened the flash drive on my tablet. It contained drafts of papers and presentations for a conference in Seattle held three years ago.

I was sure I was on the right track with Lenore. This just wasn't the right location. Calvert College. "Change your clothes," I said. "We're going to his office."

It was a short drive to campus. I parked in a dark corner of a lot. An unlit practice field laid in front of us. On the other side was the chemistry building. It was officially the middle of the night. Even those who closed the campus bars were tucked in their beds, snoring drunken Zs as we approached the back of the building. We were both dressed in black. Mine was designed to be another shadow in the night, while Hanna's was meant to get her to the front of a club line.

My private entrance to the chemistry building was as I left it. The backpack hanging off one shoulder dropped to the ground. I took a rope out of it to help cover the ten feet between me and iron.

"Why aren't we using the doors?" Hanna whispered in my ear.

"First, it being the middle of the night, they're locked. Second, this isn't exactly legal. I'll give you a boost." She went up easily, tied my rope off, and then climbed to the first landing. Using hands and feet, I scaled the distance quickly, nimbly. When I came to my full height on the landing, my lungs weren't burning, my muscles weren't singing.

Lost my edge, my ass.

Inside the building was dark, the only light coming from LEDs meant to aid in the event of emergencies. I dropped my backpack to the floor.

There was no turning on the overheads without announcing our presence. We had to make do with the wide beam of high-grade flashlights. I handed one to Hanna. "Keep the beam low." She followed my lead. Down the empty hallway. Into the cow-heavy outer office. Finally, into Damon's space.

"What the hell happened?" Hanna's beam swept across what was once treasure but was now trash. Books and papers, toys and trinkets were strewn across the floor, an apocalypse in miniature. Others had been here since Trixie and I. "Oh, Damon," she said, her voice breaking. She melted into a chair, her legs giving out. "Oh, baby."

I felt her pain, recognized it as the old friend it was. "Don't give up on him, Hanna." I went to one knee in front of her. "He's out there, waiting for us to find him."

Her eyes left me, touching on the violence behind. "This is bad. I've seen bad before, but this..." Her voice was a whisper. A tear escaped, running over her cheek to wet her lips. "How does anyone walk away from something like this?"

With a limp? But I didn't say that. She wasn't up for humor.

Instead, I put a hand on her knee. Yes, I felt her pain. Or maybe, my pain recognized hers. I expected jealousy; she had hope where I didn't. Instead, I felt a great...empathy. It was a new concept. A new feeling. Not altogether comfortable but very compelling.

"Look at me, Hanna." I waited until her eyes were on mine. "The important thing to know...is people do walk away. It's rarely easy, often messy, seldom fast, and there will be a price to pay, but people do walk away. To make sure Damon does, you and I have to be in lockstep. We have to have a singular focus on his recovery. Doubt has no place here. Do you understand me? If we are going to succeed—and we are—we live, breathe, and die knowing that we will bring Damon home."

She covered my hand. Hers trembled. "You believe?"

I shook my head. "Belief is for churches. I know." I stood and gave her an inviting smile. "Come on. We have work to do."

Hanna nodded, stood. "Where do we start?"

We sifted through the debris in the office. Nothing had escaped the destruction. A few female figures had tumbled to the floor. In a déjà vu of my time with Trixie, we brought the ceramic and glass to the table for inspection.

Hanna raised a gavel about to be repurposed as a hammer but didn't bring it down. "Thank you," she said. My face must have shown my confusion. "From the minute Damon disappeared, I was certain it was a mistake. Seeing this," she gestured to the apocalypse around us, "this isn't a mistake. This is intentional. This means Damon's kidnapping is real. It hit hard. I fell apart."

I snorted, a calculated, rude sound designed to stiffen her spine back up. "I've seen falling apart. That wasn't even close. If you want my pity, you're going to have to do better than one tear and a few gasping words. Now, are you going to work on those bat wings?"

She frowned, glanced at her tight triceps, then back at me. I bounced my eyebrows. She smiled, then smashed the bitches.

"Again!" I cheered her on. The mallet struck true, fracturing and then shattering the rigid materials until the figures' secrets were laid out before us.

"There's nothing here." Hanna ran her fingers through the chards. "Damn."

I was at a loss. Every alley was a dead end. "Everything related to Poe or ravens or Lenore has been reduced to its simplest elements."

Elements.

In chemistry, elements were the fundamentals, those basic substances that could not be broken down into anything simpler. This was different than how I used the word, meaning the scraps of paper, wood, and metal were now nothing more than trash. But. I swung my light to the closed door. "His lab."

The lab had escaped with the equivalent of bumps and bruises. With the tabletop tools of a chemist being largely transparent, the treasure hunters hadn't spent the time on their destruction.

"Whoever was in here was a professional," I said. "There's no hate or anger. Just business."

"I have a thing or two to say about their business." Hanna had a dark side I appreciated. She held her anger in check, barely, as she sorted through the open cabinets and the contents vomited on the floor. More books. Boxes, jars, and bags. The refrigerator marked "not for edibles" was messy, but nothing was broken.

Standing with my back to the hallway door, I swept the light around the room. Above the whiteboards, a clock hung unviolated. Also untouched were the elements on the periodic table, the continuum of the nerdy picture frame on Hanna's desk. "Damon loves his elements, doesn't he?"

She chuckled. "Yes. He is obsessed with them as with Poe."

Suddenly, my heart raced. "Could it be that easy? Could it be as obvious as HElium, RhEnium, Iodine, and AMericium?"

Hanna turned away from her work. "What are you talking about?"

"HERE. I. AM." I pointed to the boxes circling the room. "If I was going to spell Lenore using elements, it would be...LIthium, Nitrogen, Oxygen, RhEnium. LINORE. What do you think? Close enough?"

"Only one way to find out." She stalked to the wall, snagging a stool as she passed. She climbed. She balanced. She had her hands on the prize when the sound of steps came from the hall. They were slow, careful little taps of heels. This wasn't a grad student coming in at four in the morning.

"Down. Hide." I gave the order and snatched the fire extinguisher. With weapon in hand, I paced along with the steps on the other side of the wall, trusting Hanna found cover.

A door opened, then shut. The outer door to Damon's office.

Another did the same, the sound coming through the adjoining door. A click, and yellow light imitating day poured across the lab.

Somebody had balls.

I expected the somebody to enter my territory and turn on the lights. I readied the extinguisher, aiming for average height and ready to adjust.

"No respect," the interloper muttered. The voice was male; I raised my aim. Noise came of the debris being moved, perhaps a path being cleared. "Annalisa, I know you're here."

"Diamond," I said as I set the extinguisher on the table. "Trevor, what are you doing here?"

He stepped into the lab, turning on the light and freaking blinding me. "Me? What are you doing here? Nice to see your eyes, but what happened to your hair?"

"Trev, you're lighting us up like the fourth of July. Turn the lights off. This is my hair. My real hair."

"Always knew you weren't a natural blonde." He crossed his arms, moving to block the light switch. "I'm allowed to be here, they're staying on. You came in the fire escape, didn't you?"

I could see him now, the figure of irritated authority. "I like to think of it as my private entrance. Hanna, come on out."

Trevor's attitude softened when he recognized the woman climbing from under a table. "Hanna. What are you doing hanging out with trouble like Diamond?"

"Looking for Damon, what else? The police won't help." She held her position, the table in front of her, with her chin up, eyes determined. "This place looks horrible. What's happened?"

"There have been two break-ins. Well, three. I've personally taken on the assignment to guard this floor. What?" he asked in response to me growling like a dog. "Don't think I'm up to it?"

"I told you, these people are ruthless. You won't be anything but an obstacle. They will take you out without thought. No kissing your wife in the morning. No tucking your kids in at night. Nothing in your future but satin and oak." I snapped out each word, being as brutal as I could to get through to the dumb fuck.

He lifted his chin in defiance but swallowed one time too many for a man with no regard for his life. "There's nothing here. They'll get the message and stop."

"They won't believe it until they see for themselves. And there is something here."

"You're kidding. What? Where?"

I pointed to the box above the stool. "I need lithium."

"You're telling me," he muttered as he looked to Hanna. "You buying this?"

Hanna lifted her chin. "We need lithium."

Muttering about crazy women, Trevor climbed, easily lifting the element off the hanger. He handed it down to me.

I examined the wood box of the frame. The lettering was screened onto canvas, which was pulled tight across a supporting block. Taking a knife from my boot, I separated the top of the wood frame from the back along a flat seam. It was a slow process, breaking the glue and removing the corners millimeter by millimeter. I was prepared to find nothing but the guts of geek art. Careful as I was, lithium would never go back together again.

Hanna stood with me, eyes glued to our project. Trevor

stood over her shoulder.

The frame gapped now. Hanna pressed her fingers into the space. Together, we made the final separation. She examined the frame pieces while I worked on the canvas. It peeled reluctantly from the thick piece of wood that had given it form. The wood was a single piece of balsa, without seams, cuts, or other imperfections. Inspecting the canvas revealed a silky pouch. From within, I pulled a handwritten page.

"'When I had journeyed half of our life's way,'" I read, "'I found myself within a shadowed forest for I had lost the path that does not stray. Turn away.' Great, just what I needed. A riddle."

"It's a warning," Trevor said. "I think the first line is from Dante's *Inferno*. Have you read it?" I shook my head. Hanna did the same. "It's an old story, a classic. Dante finds himself in a forest, lost. It's figurative. He was lost on his life's journey, which he paralleled with being physically lost."

I held up my hand. I did not have time for a lecture in literature. "How does he get out?"

He got that look people get when they feel sorry for how little you understand of something they think is fundamental to being educated. "He goes through hell." The "duh" went unspoken. "Damon is warning us not to continue. Look at it. This isn't paper. It's papyrus."

"That's still a thing?" Leave it to a scientist to use an ancient medium for a next-generation weapon. "Screw his warning. We wouldn't have to do this at all if he didn't go and get himself kidnapped. We need nitrogen, oxygen, and rhenium."

Trevor made quick work of the task. We laid them on the table, ready to open them in order, of course. We had to be more careful than we felt. We didn't know the condition or even the location of the messages. I wasn't certain where they were concealed within the frames. Damon had been deliberate about his work. I wouldn't put it past him to embed some compound that would disintegrate the papyrus.

It's what I would have done.

As well as planting a few other surprises, just to discourage Nosey Nancies.

Point being, this wasn't your high school science project. My gaze slid to Hanna. Damon belonged to Hanna and so Hanna belonged here. But Trevor. "Go home, Trev. Forget everything you saw."

"Not happening. Damon was my friend. I stay." He scanned the room, ignoring the immovable object in front of him, i.e., me. "There's gotta be another knife around here." He rummaged through drawers, silent until he found two. "You can waste our time bitching, or we can get to work." He handed one to Hanna.

She accepted. "Let's get to work."

"Stubborn man. Fine. Have it your way." I made use of both of them. I would think about covering Trevor's ass later. Another thirty minutes and three more pages were lying on the table.

"Do you understand these?" he asked.

Hanna picked up one of the pages. "I can read his writing but don't understand what he wrote. It might as well be in Greek."

"When I was his grad student, I was fully literate in Damon's shorthand, but it's been years. Let me see...these are definitely directions." I traced the words with my finger, reaching into the far recesses of my mind. With every word, direction, compound I remembered a little more. My excitement rose. Damn, but I loved this. I studied each page. The last made me laugh out loud.

"What?" Trevor demanded, leaning so far over my shoulder he rested his chin on my collar bone.

"Damon was tricky here. It looks like these should go two, three, four, right? Nitrogen, oxygen, rhenium. The last line of the rhenium page switches the order." In the lower-right corner was a doodle.

"What is that?" Hanna asked. "Some kinda fish?"

"A bass, swimming backwards. Bass-ackwards. One of Damon's favorite expressions, but if you didn't know him, you would miss the direction." I drummed my fingers. This was why he was kidnapped. This was what everyone was looking for. We had it.

But how to use it.

There hadn't been a ransom. Yes, a threat was carved into Hanna's table, but there was no means to contact the assholes, almost as though there was no expectation Hanna could deliver. So, was this all a red herring? A sleight of hand to distract me from the real action? Was Damon being held in a lab somewhere, forced to re-create the solution? If so, he had a better chance of being alive.

The formula gave me something to trade, but to really get an edge...Damon's lab was that of a working chemist, of an inventing chemist.

"I don't like that look in your eye." Trevor snapped me out of my thoughts.

My mouth curled wryly. He sounded like my mother. "I have some work to do. Alone. Take Hanna back to my place, then go home, Trevor. Crawl in bed with your wife, make love to her. Stay on the path that does not stray."

Hanna crossed her arms under her breasts. "I'm not leaving. If you have work, then I have work."

Trevor stared at me. I saw the moment he understood. What I was going to do next, if I succeeded, when I succeeded, people would kill for. "This is crazy." He pressed his lips together, thin and tight, in the piercing stare of his gaze. "Don't do it."

"If not me, then who?" I took his hand, looked in his eyes so he felt my resolve. "Don't waste your energy worrying about me. I was made for this."

His nod was reluctant. "I'll keep everyone away from here. I'll come back tomorrow with food for the both of you and something to cover the windows." He went all stubborn man when I shook my head. "Don't argue with me, Annalisa. You can't do this alone. Give me your cell number. I'll text you when I'm coming back."

"Annalisa? Is that your real name?" Hanna smiled softly.

"It's pretty."

"Diamond," I said as I texted him. "My real name is Diamond."

Trevor exited, leaving me with Hanna. "You're going to make this..." She waved her hand at the pages spread before us. "...thing."

"Whoever has Damon wants this 'thing.' We make it, we have the ultimate leverage."

"Then what are we waiting for? Tell me what you want me to do."

"Let's start with the first line." Getting into the espionage business had taken me far from the laboratory. My brain was rusty when it came to chemistry, especially at this level, but it would come back to me.

Give me a moment.

Any minute now.

"Problem?" Hanna asked.

"Not a problem. I just need to, you know, warm up, so to speak." I really needed to tap some resources. There were other professors in this department, new grad students, someone who could read this.

But. But, but, but. Someone was killing for this information. Anyone helping me would be painting a target on their back. I sent Trevor away because of it. I wasn't bitch enough to pull someone else in.

In the time it took for the hands on the clock to tick-tock-tick to five in the morning, we made pathetically little progress. Hanna dozed on the couch in the office. She was a good assistant, supportive without being intrusive, but this wasn't her field. Rubbing my eyes, I considered abandoning the project. I didn't need the actual product if I had the formula. Re-creating the compound added leverage, sure, and maybe I was a little curious after the conversation with Jeremy Hardy...

Jeremy Hardy!

He had been there at the formula's origin. He had worked on

the first generation. And, bonus, he already had a target on his back. If I didn't take care of this, sooner or later, he'd be dead. It would only help him if he helped me. In fact, he should beg me to help.

I dug out my phone and woke up my newest employee.

"'Ello?"

"Elliot, Diamond. Got a job for you. Do you remember where you took Jeremy?"

"The guy? Sure," he said, breaking through the cobwebs in his voice. "I remember."

"Go grab him and bring him to the chemistry building at Calvert College. How long do you think it will take?"

"Calvert? Let me think, maybe three hours."

"You got two. Another two grand, minus fifty bucks for every minute late." I ended the call before he could argue.

Knowing help was on the way kickstarted my brain. When my phone rang two hours and fourteen minutes later, Hanna was back on her feet and we had worked through the directions under rhenium and were solidly into oxygen. "Talk to me, Elliot."

"Driving through the big stone towers now."

"Follow the road to the left." I directed him through campus to the cargo bay on the side of the building. Hanna and I met him there, watching an SUV that screamed "Soccer Dad" make the final turn toward the building.

"If this is one of the scientists from Germany," she said, "we could always trade him for Damon. You know, if we can't reproduce the Raven."

I looked at Hanna to see if it was a joke, 'cause her voice wasn't laughing. Neither was her face. Like I said, she had a dark side. "Well, it's good to have options, but we'll get this done." I climbed down as the car turned off. "Nice SUV."

"Your friend Black sent me to a place. They set me up, just like he said." He opened the rear door.

"Did you have...why is he tied up?" Jeremy was in the back seat, trussed up like a Thanksgiving turkey.

"You said grab him. So, I did."

"Damn it, but you need to get your head out of the Fast and Furious movies." Jeremy's wrists were bound with thick, silver duct tape and a long piece was pressed across his mouth. "Get out of there. Hanna, find some scissors." I pulled the tape off Jeremy's mouth.

"You fucking asshole!" Jeremy lunged at Elliot using his wadded-up hands as a club.

Elliot spun, taking the blows on his back. "Not my fault, I just did what she said."

Jeremy turned on me. I shrugged and walked to the door, leaving them to follow. "Let's get inside. The police have an auxiliary office on the back of the building."

"Asshole," Jeremy said again as he stalked away from his abductor.

Elliot closed the rear door. "Can I go? My kid has a soccer game at nine thirty."

"Sure. I'll call you when Jeremy is ready to leave."

"No," Jeremy said.

"You're the boss," Elliot said chipperly, climbing into the driver's seat. "I have soccer games at nine thirty and noon and then baseball games at two and four thirty."

Jeremy crossed his arms. Well, he tried to. "I'm not getting back in a car with that maniac."

Elliot looked at me, sincerity in his face. "I'll make it work, even if I have to shove him in the trunk."

"That's what I'm afraid of. I'll Uber it. Hell, I'll walk before I let you drive me anywhere. Ever."

"Relax," I said, ushering Jeremy into the building. "He's being figurative. The SUV doesn't have a trunk."

"What the hell am I doing here? And who is she?"

"She is Hanna, Damon Marten's, uh, wife." Really, it was just easier. "We need help," I said as Hanna began snipping at the tape. "The compound you made in Germany—"

"Serum," he corrected, holding his flipper out. "What

about it?"

"We found the formula, but my chemistry skills are a little rusty. Need your expert help."

"Are you crazy?"

Do I butt into his personal life? "Not clinically. Does it matter?"

"That was rhetorical. I know you're crazy if you're trying to re-create a disaster. What are you thinking?" He pulled his hands apart, but the tape held.

"Is that rhetorical, too?"

"No. What thought is your pea-sized brain processing to think this, in any way, could be a good idea?" He redirected to Hanna. "You're in on this, too?"

"We need leverage," she said. "If there was another way, we'd do it. If there is a chance to bring Damon home, then I'm in."

"It's about keeping you and China alive," I said. "We need something the bad guys want more than they want you. We have the formula. That's something. A big something. But how would they know it's the real thing? As long as they wonder or doubt, the target is on your back."

Jeremy stepped away from us, peeling the rest of the tape from his hands with his teeth. He freed one thumb, then the other. In quick order, he was ambidextrous again. "I do this, and you become a target. I can't live with that."

"I'm doing this with or without your—"

"—we," Hanna said, cutting me off. "I don't understand chemistry the way you do. With you, Diamond will be faster and maybe Damon lives. He was your friend once, can you live with turning your back on him?"

Jeremy swore softly, she nearly had him. I pushed all-in.

"If you can help us, great. If you can't, I'll get you out of here, get you back into hiding for however long this takes."

He huffed like a bull, swinging his head between us and the door.

"Just, take a look. That's all I'm asking."

“Fine, I’ll look. I’m not promising anything.” Once Jeremy saw the formulas, he was hooked. “You’re on the right track. He’s made changes since I left. Yes, I remember.”

The work was trial and error as we deciphered the past, using the formula as a guide. Every time a piece dropped into place, it was like hitting the lottery. We pushed each other harder, further. When one of us lagged, the others carried. We slept in shifts. Trevor came and went, bringing bags of food and thick, black plastic sheets to cover the windows.

In the middle of Saturday night, the path forward was as obvious as an airport runway. At least to me.

“I can’t figure out his shorthand here.” Jeremy was bent over the table, his nose inches from the paper.

I was in my backpack, taking a small envelope from the concealed pocket. “Give me a minute. I’ll take a look.” The powder from the envelope went into two bottles of water. “This is thirsty work. Need some?”

“Thanks.” He drank heartily. “This is the part he’s changed. I think we supercooled the solution. It doesn’t look like he did that. And what is he adding?” He rubbed his eyes. “I’m not sure it’s in English.”

“Maybe. Hanna, water?”

“This is harder work than it seems.” She drank half the bottle. “What can I do next?”

We worked for ten more minutes before both were swaying on their feet. “You guys need some sleep? Go ahead and catch some shut-eye. I can keep going.”

Jeremy yawned so wide, his jaw cracked. “It just came out of nowhere. I was fine a minute ago.”

“Stop it,” Hanna chastised, yawning herself. “You’re making me do it.”

The two shuffled into the office. Soon, Jeremy snored in Damon’s chair. Hanna crashed on the couch. Me? I unearthed the final ingredient. A hallucinogenic. Why couldn’t Jeremy identify it? It was in English, but in a slang that made sense only in these four walls. It proved not only that this was Damon's work but that he created it within the last ten years.

I zeroed out a scale and then began pouring. A small pile of powder grew until the scale read the needed weight. Stirring the solution gently, I poured the powder in.

Crystals began growing, at first so small I doubted what my eyes saw. With each rotation of the stirring rod, the delicate structures increased in size and complexity. It was like watching the birth of a snowflake, shining structures reaching out, creating detailed lattices.

Where one structure met another, the networks connected, becoming thicker. Translucent beauty gave way to solid, white geometric shapes. Cubes and pyramids, prisms and tetrahedrons jutted in all directions, pushing the remaining fluid to the outside. The reaction continued, gobbling up the liquid, pushing the white diamonds into the glass and up toward the top lip. With a gloved hand, I lifted the beaker and slid a plate beneath it, concerned the expansion could break the glass.

The reaction slowed as the last visible liquid morphed into a solid. I waited as though listening for the last kernel of popcorn to pop.

Satisfied the work of chemistry was completed, I studied what I had made. The glass was satisfyingly warm. I felt it through the gloves I wore as I lifted it to the light. The angles and planes reflected the white light into the color spectrum. I turned it slowly, smiling at the kaleidoscope of blues, yellows, and greens flashing brilliantly before hiding again beneath the white façade.

I returned to the last portion of the directions, the ones hidden under nitrogen. This step would dissolve the crystal and reveal the deadly prize.

I pried a quarter of the crystal into a glass flask. The remainder was wrapped securely within a box and buried at the bottom of my pack.

Then I woke Jeremy and Hanna.

We stood in a corner, shoulder to shoulder, the only sound the fan of the air filter system. Even our breath was silent through the respirators we wore. On the table, just ten feet in front of us, amber fluid dripped from a condenser.

Liquid gold.

"Look familiar?" I asked Jeremy quietly. The moment was one of those best with hushed voices.

Jeremy nodded, slowly, reverently. "We need to test it." He snapped out of the amazement that bemused us, looking around for a victim. "What I wouldn't give for a rat right now."

"Yeah. Or a robin. A flock of them."

Hanna looked at me like I was weird. "What would it do, if we had a rat?"

"The drug combination will act as an inhibitor, disrupting the communication between the brain stem, cerebellum, and frontal lobe. The subject will lose coordination, balance, ability to move."

"Does it hurt?"

"No. Of course not. We designed this to help people, not hurt them. There's nothing in the formula to cause pain. It just temporarily stops parts of the brain from talking to other parts."

It was a good idea. I could count on fingers and toes the number of times something like Raven could have helped me. "Thank you, Jeremy. You do good work. Tell me how to handle testing it, and I'll get your ride."

"I am not letting Elliot the Idiot drive me anywhere." He rubbed his eyes. "My cousin has a cabin in Upstate New York I can use. There wouldn't be a paper trail. I just need a car and money for groceries."

"Consider it done. Let me make a call."

I went into Damon's office, dug out my phone, then rang Ian.

"Thought you fell off the face of the Earth."

"Not yet. I cracked Damon's code, with a little help from friends. I have both the formula and a few ounces of the serum. We have leverage, Ian. Now we just need to get a hold of the people holding Damon."

"We've had some progress over here, too. Dix is piecing together surveillance footage. We have Damon from the college to a hotel near Dulles Airport. He's working on sharpening the images. I've tracked back through the contact Elliot fed me and came up with a name: Leo Krause."

I smiled, a lioness ready to render anything stupid enough to cross my path. "Good work. I need you to arrange for a car and cash to last someone a month."

"You need it now, I assume."

"You assume correctly." With Ian on the task of making Jeremy disappear, I returned to the laboratory. "Let's put this place back like we found it."

My phone lit up. A text from Trevor. "Hey Jeremy, found those rats you were hoping for."

EVERY ACTION NEEDS AN EXOTHERMIC REACTION

I hummed as I worked. This was going to be fun. The two fortune hunters heading this way were going to find exactly what they were looking for. And after, Trevor was going to be a hero for catching the perps. Oh yes, this was going to be a good day. Jeremy and Hanna stood in the doorway, watching as I set an inconspicuous camera in position on a shelf, angled to cover the office door and the rest of the room. A second camera came out of the backpack and went on another shelf. This one was at the opposite end of the room, catching what the first camera missed. "And, the trap is set. Get back into the lab."

"You sure this is going to work?" Jeremy cast his doubt on the small glass jar lying next to a box as though it had fallen out. The black lid had a wide strip of masking tape across it with the instructions handwritten by yours truly.

"Never doubt the power of curiosity." I shouldered my pack and ushered the two of them back into the lab, heretofore known as our control room. A few swipes on my smartphone and we had full view of the office. The sun had risen, nicely lighting the scene.

Soft footfalls approached.

I quickly positioned the adjoining door open enough to hear the performers without being seen. The three of us were under one of the heavy tables, invisible should curious eyes gaze our way. My phone was on the floor, propped against a table leg.

"The door's wide open." The voice was male, with a cadence found on the wrong side of tracks everywhere. We'll call him City Rat.

Another voice grunted. It was deep, low. "We aren't the first." This male voice had a twist to his vowels that did not come from the US of A. The accent wasn't distinct enough, in those few words, to determine origin. Eastern European was my first guess. We'll call him Euro Rat. "Shut the door."

A sharp but quiet click came. The outer office door was closed.

A man stepped into the dual camera feeds. Average height, thick build. Short hair swept back from his forehead. He wore a suit. He sighed. "We are not the first," Euro Rat said, stepping fully into the room. He began to his right, away from the lab, sifting through the debris.

"Shit." City Rat stood inside the door, shaking his head. He was taller than his partner, lanky. He, too, wore a suit. "Waste of our time. If there was anything here, it's long gone."

"Maybe. Maybe not. Everyone else is looking for a raven, a bird. We are looking for a different kind of raven, a poem."

"I heard what Karl said. I just didn't understand it." City Rat stepped forward, head sweeping left and right over the pile of books, papers, and office trinkets. He held up the broken cock stick. "That's just wrong."

I looked at Jeremy and silently mouthed the name City Rat shared. Karl. Jeremy shook his head. Hanna looked like some kind of carnival doll, eyes too big for her face. Normal people get scared when they're hiding under tables, I reminded myself. I gave her a thumbs-up, a question.

She nodded, swallowing hard. God, she better not throw up.

"Wonder what this is?" City Rat picked up the jar containing a hastily made infusion of petroleum jelly and the Raven serum.

"What does it say? On the top."

"'Keep Closed.'" He set it up on an empty shelf, uninterested.

Jeremy elbowed me and whispered, "It's not going to work."

"Just wait," I whispered back. No one had patience anymore.

Euro Rat picked up book after book, thumbing through them for text other than the scientific variety, shaking each one for loose pages. City Rat began doing the same. There were a lot of books on the floor. Neither rat was daunted by the task, systematically searching the textbooks, paperbacks, and three-ring binders. They created stacks of the completed ones, cleaning the room as they searched.

Watching someone search for something you know isn't there has the excitement of watching paint dry…or water boil…of doing taxes…of peeling wallpaper…of, of, of—

Jeremy elbowed me again, pointing to the screen. Euro Rat held the jar, turning it to inspect it from all sides. Then his hand closed over the top.

"What are you doin'?" City Rat asked. "It says keep closed."

"So?"

"So, someone put that on there for a reason."

"Like what?"

"Like maybe it explodes when air touches it."

Euro Rat paused to consider. "No," he said with an accompanying shake of his head. "No one would keep explosives in such a little jar." He opened it. He sniffed it. He threw his head back, turning his nose away. "This stinks. Smell it." He held it out toward City Rat.

"Get that shit away from me. What you thinkin' tellin' me it stinks and then to smell it? Ain't like I can't smell it from here."

Euro Rat turned back to the Raven, dipping in the tip of a gloved finger. He rubbed it between his thumb and index finger, brought it again to his nose, and then, oh wow, he touched his index finger to his tongue.

Jeremy stared at the screen with wide eyes. He shook his head, his breathing speeding up. "He can't do that," he said in a loud whisper. "We never tested it for ingestion." He brought a knee in, leaned toward the aisle to climb out.

I knocked his leg out from under him, pinning him to the floor. I caught his head in a hold that put me in charge. "It's too late. Going out there will just get you killed. Stay quiet or I'll put you out. Understand?" I tightened my hold, cutting off his air to show him I was serious.

We returned our attention to the screen. Euro Rat put the jar back on the shelf, lid in place. He squatted down, returning to the drudgery of searching the books.

My heart raced with anticipation to see if this formula did what Jeremy claimed, if it was worth killing for, if it was worth dying for.

Euro Rat giggled.

I wouldn't have thought a man with a neck as thick as his could giggle, but he did.

He did it again. I looked to Jeremy, silently asking if that was normal. Jeremy shrugged.

City Rat glanced over his shoulder. "Something funny?"

Euro Rat sprung from his squat, landing three feet to the side.

"What the fuck are you doin'?"

Euro Rat snickered again. "I'm over here."

If this was a graphic novel, there would have been a dozen question marks around City Rat's head. And mine. Jeremy's too. Hanna's three.

"I know you over there," City Rat said, his voice climbing.

"No, you don't. You can't see me." He raised his arm, palm out and fingers spread wide. "I'm invisible."

"The fuck you are," City Rat said, kneeling to face his partner. "You are right there. I can see you."

"You can't see me." Euro Rat raced through the words.

"Yes, I can." City Rat carefully enunciated each of his.

"No, you can't."

"Yes. I can." City Rat rose to his feet. "What the hell you talkin' 'bout? I can see you. You are right there." He emphasized his point with a finger to Euro Rat's shoulder.

Euro Rat looked down at his hands, then back up to City Rat. "It's the suit." And he started to strip. Suit coat. Shoulder harness and gun. Tie. Dress shirt. Clothing was removed head to toe while City Rat ran behind the hip-high desk for protection.

"What the fuck are you doin'? Stop. Don't take that belt off. I'm serious. This ain't no place to get nekkid. Get your hands off your fly."

"You can't see my hands."

"Yes. I. Can. You aren't fucking invisible!"

Euro Rat was naked. He danced around the clean space the two had made, waving his arms up and down. He made a large circle, then came around for a second, swooping close to City Rat, who had his gun pulled.

"What the hell is wrong with you! Stop this shit."

Euro Rat didn't stop. He didn't seem to realize there was anyone else in the room. Stopping in the center, he threw back his head and cawed. Then his arms began flailing again, his "flight" becoming faster, out of control. He bounced off a wall and kicked over the stack of books. Around and around he went without care of anything in his path. One bare foot planted on the pages of an open book. The book slid under the weight, putting Euro Rat into a bookcase. The few books remaining on the shelves were pulled down as he fell. In the time it took to blink, the naked man sprawled across the floor, his head and shoulders propped at an uncomfortable angle.

I released Jeremy, sliding to the floor next to him. "Look at City Rat."

"Who? You mean the other guy? He's just sitting there."

The second camera showed City Rat on the floor, his back against the desk, legs extended, feet flopped apart. His arms hung heavy, hands on the ground as though they stayed where they had fallen. The gun sat on his open palm. "This is some kind of messed up. I did not sign up for this. Nope. 'Simple job,' they said. 'Just need to find a black bird,' they said. Nobody said nothin' about nekkid shit." The stream of conscious thought flowed uninhibited. City Rat was utterly calm, speaking without inflection.

"I'm going in." I climbed out from under cover and strapped on the mask I'd worn when I filled the jar with Raven. "Stay behind here." I entered the office, sighting my gun on City Rat.

"Never liked Glocks," he said. "Not a fan of the trigger."

Gotta admit, I didn't know what to say to that. Usually when I walk in a room with my weapon drawn, it's "Don't shoot" or "He went out the window" or "Armed women turn me on," not a criticism of my weapon.

He didn't make a move toward his gun, a Smith & Wesson tactical model. In fact, he didn't move below the neck. I used my foot to clear the gun from his hand. He never flinched.

"How you feeling?" I asked, trying to gauge the situation.

"Fine, just fine. You?"

Like we were at a garden party. "I'm good. Who are you?"

"Napoleon Caesar Churchill."

I snorted. Couldn't help it. "You're making that up."

"I wish I was. You know what it's like growing up with a name like that? Shit. I was twenty before I got laid. Can't impress women with no name like that."

"No, I guess you can't." I squatted to bring us eye to eye. His pupils were large black pools rimmed with narrow bands of brown. The morning light had to be killing his head, bright as it was. "What are you doing here, Napoleon?"

"Oh, on some dumbass wild goose chase looking for a bird with a formula for some top-secret chemical warfare thingy." His voice was calm as a still lake.

"Thingy?" This guy was priceless. I heard a door open and glanced over my shoulder to find Jeremy and Hanna, both with masks.

Jeremy's face was stern beneath the filtering mask. "It's acting like a truth serum. The guy is so relaxed, he has no filter. Ask him something else."

I asked what mattered most. "Who hired you?"

"Karl," Napoleon said without hesitation. "He's paying top dollar, too. My man Mirko there, he went to school with Karl, says he's one fucked up son-of-a-bitch, turned out just like his daddy, but pays his bills. You wouldn't believe how many people will hire you to do their dirty work, then try to stiff you."

"You're kidding."

"I am not. 'Oh, Napoleon, my boss is prick,'" he said in a whiney falsetto, "'I'll pay you a C-note to slash his tires,' which I do. Do you think I got the cash?"

"No?"

"Damn right, no. Bitch offers me a blow job instead. Can't spend a blow job at the grocery store, you get me?"

"I get you. Tell me more about Karl."

"Don't know no more about Karl. Mirko, you tell her about Karl. That's nasty, Mirko. Why you doing that?" Which got the three of us turning to the naked man.

Mirko's chest was rising and falling with rapid, shallow crests. His fingers were swollen sausages with joints too puffy to bend. His blue irises were awash in a sea of pink that darkened by the second. Blood red tears welling in the corners of his eyes spilled over, leaving a macabre trail down his cheeks.

"Why you got a mask on? You, too?" Napoleon babbled on about masks and whatever came to his drugged-out mind. His voice was falling on deaf ears.

"Oh, dear God." Jeremy whispered the words, a plea for mercy where science had none. "What did we do?"

"What's going on?" Hanna asked. "Is that supposed to happen?"

"No," Jeremy said. "He must be overdosing. It wasn't meant to be ingested or inhaled at a high concentration."

I removed my glove, pressing my fingers to Mirko's neck. His pulse was rapid, nearly too fast to count.

"Overdosing? Mirko doesn't do drugs," Napoleon said. "He's all about holistic shit and meditating. You know he has his own organic farm?"

Mirko was crying blood. How do you undo that?

A harsh, sliding sound made me turn. Jeremy was throwing open the windows. "We need to air this room out." He slipped on a book, nearly falling, fighting to get to the next window. "Get masks for Napoleon and Mirko."

"I don't think..." I caught myself, recognizing the frantic need Jeremy had to right the wrong we'd done. "Hanna, help me get Napoleon into the lab."

Working together, we dragged his boneless body into the clean air. Jeremy tore down the tarp covering the windows, shoving the glass beneath open. I checked Napoleon's pulse. It was elevated but not dangerous, no faster than my own at that moment.

Jeremy retrieved two masks from the cabinet in the lab. He fit the first over Napoleon. "Breathe deep and slow."

Napoleon grinned widely. "You look like a teacher. You a teacher?"

"No," Jeremy said without elaboration.

"Well, you should be. This is a laboratory, ain't it?"

"Yes. I'm going to check on your friend. Just stay put." Jeremy patted his shoulder.

Napoleon's fingers twitched. Hopefully, it was a sign the lethargy was wearing off. "He's dead, you know that. Saw something like that down in Nawlins when I was a kid. My mama's aunt was a voodoo priestess—she made a man cry blood." His feet jerked in short, random ways. "His daddy buried him the next day on holy grounds to make sure he stay dead." He turned his head toward me. "You got some eyes on you. You a voodoo priestess?"

"Not today." I checked his eyes. They were dilated, but his whites were still white. "How you feeling?"

"Getting the pins and needles in my hands and feet."

"That's a good sign," I told him, hoping it was. "I'll be back."

In the office, Jeremy stood solemnly over a horrific corpse. Hanna had her back pressed against the wall, a hand over her appalled face. Fluids of all natures oozed from Euro Rat's body. By the smell, the bowels had let go. I picked up the suit coat and draped it over Mirko's head and chest.

"We're monsters," Jeremy whispered.

Hanna was on the verge of crying. "Why would Damon create something like this?" Her blue eyes, swimming in tears, locked on me. Hard.

"You can't let them have it," Jeremy said. "What are we going to do?"

No, I couldn't trade Raven for Damon. Damn it. I was better off not knowing what Raven did. Then I could have made a deal, in good conscience. One thing was clear. "We can't leave anything for others to find. Until this Karl is satisfied, they'll keep coming, and maybe one of them is smart enough to put it all together. It needs to end here, with us."

Hanna shook her head. It was on a nonstop swivel, like a battery-operated bobblehead. She was pale, the healthy rose gone from her cheeks. She ran back into the lab and vomited into the first sink.

"Go help her," I told Jeremy. "I need to stage the room. The fire investigators need a scapegoat."

"The whole room needs to burn. Hot." Jeremy saw to Hanna, then went to work with a chemical whose secondary properties made it a particularly nasty accelerant.

"You need a nozzle. You know, something to get that shit into the cracks. You just dabbin'. How's that supposed to work?" Napoleon had turned into a filibustering color commentator. "Hey! Look at me! I told my fingers to move and they did." He stared at his hand, cackling when his thumb made a slow circle.

"We're clear," I said, zipping my backpack closed.

"Where's the serum?" Jeremy asked. "I want to soak it good. We can't have any of it left in the air when the firefighters come in."

I shook my head. "You aren't thinking it through. We burn it, we release it into the air. There's a campus full of kids around us.

It's safer to take it with us."

He stopped his work, turning slowly until he faced me. "You want to keep it." His gaze met mine, color creeping into his face. "Are you insane! You saw what it did to that man." He spoke with a white-hot fury, a bellowing voice of reason. "No one should have access to this kind of power. Absolute power corrupts absolutely. It can't exist. Get it while I set up the burner."

He wasn't wrong.

But...everything on this earth has the potential to heal as much as to kill. Many medicines and antidotes are lethal at high-enough doses. Hello, can you say opiates? Every part of a Yew tree is toxic. If burned, the smoke can make you sick, but extracted compounds are used in some cancer medications. Hell, a friend of mine was getting dosed with rat poison for his heart condition.

And we just worked for days on this. Literal days. Throwing it away would be like flushing time down the toilet. Time is too precious to be flushed.

"Bring it over here," Jeremy demanded. He had the blue flame burning high.

He wasn't going to take no for an answer. I dug in my backpack, pulled out the jar Mirko had sniffed, and handed it over. He didn't know about the crystal. Neither did Hanna.

"Ready to go, Napoleon?" I went to our newest friend and helped him to his feet. He was a marionette without strings, his limbs useless without a puppet master. "Hanna, help. He can't walk. We need to do this together if we're going to get him out."

"If him has a say, him votes yes, get him out." Napoleon's arm hung limply around my neck. "Get your pretty ass over here, Hanna."

Between the two of us, Napoleon's skinny ass was easy enough to handle. His feet dragged behind, unable to keep up with our pace. His mouth worked overtime to make up for his legs. "It's like my body went to the dentist and now I can't drink without drooling. But it's not like Mirko. That was some kind of messed up. Yo, I didn't sign up for this shit."

Hanna and I struggled down the stairs, his dragging legs throwing us off balance.

"I should have known better, taking a job at a college. I tried it, you know. Wasn't for me. Come to think of it, I was carried out then, too."

And then Jeremy caught up. "Go, go, go, go." He took Hanna's place, and we raced down the steps. When Jeremy would have headed for the front door, I pulled the pair toward a corner. "To the loading dock. I took the camera out down there. We can't be seen."

Around the corner, and my favorite average white man was coming our way.

"Diamond." Ian stopped, did a one-eighty, and smacked the button to open the double doors he'd just come through. "Trouble behind you?"

"Fire in the hole. Where's your car?"

"Outside the door." He shoved me out of the way, taking Napoleon's weight. "You hurt?"

I shook him off, straightening from where I'd bent over to catch my breath. "We need to get away from here. Now." I raced ahead to the man door, holding it open for the trio. "Keys," I shouted. Ian tossed them. I had the engine running before they got to the car. With Jeremy, Napoleon, and Hanna in the back, Ian jumped into the front seat. He closed the door as we peeled up the wide drive.

"Damn, look at her burn." Napoleon's neck was starting to work. "You ever see anything like that?"

I glanced over my shoulder. Thick black smoke billowed from the third-floor windows. Fire licked the floor above with tongues of red, yellow, and killer white. An explosion and shattering glass punctuated the morning. Two more explosions followed, a quick *pop-pop*, nearly indistinguishable from gunfire.

Answering sirens raced in from the north. The lights were lost behind the long building that screened us from sight. We could hear the sound of the firefight from the parking spot next to my car.

"Jeremy, you know the rules. Stay out of sight until I finish this. No calls to the office. No logging into your email. No using your credit card. Think recluse. It'll keep you alive."

He nodded, accepting an envelope Ian handed back. "Thanks."

"Oh, once this is over, call Natasha, the cupcake lady. I promised her you'd call after the emergency at the factory is over."

"Natasha. Right. Thanks for the cover. You'll call when it's over, right? I'd like to have lunch again."

"What about my lunch?" Napoleon leaned forward, showing the strength he was regaining. "You can't leave me here. I can't walk. And what happens when Karl comes? You leave me and I'll tell him everything I know."

I snorted. "You don't know anything. And what are you doing? Trying to give me a reason to kill you?"

"What?! Who said anything about killing? No killing. It is off the table." He turned to Jeremy. "Take me with you. You owe me. I can't walk because of you. I might never walk again because of you. Take me with you and we'll call it even."

Gotta give Napoleon credit. He saw guilt in Jeremy's face and played him like a banjo. Actually, it wasn't a bad idea. I had to do something with Napoleon to keep him from talking to the wrong people.

Ten minutes later, Jeremy sat in the late model car with a new license plate, a burner phone, and double the cash. Napoleon was in the passenger seat, using his still non-articulating hand to tune the radio. "We'll text you when we get there," Jeremy said.

"Let me know if anyone tries to contact you. Either of you. We'll cover your back." I rapped on the hood, stepping back to let him pull out. Ian did the same in my car, Hanna in the back seat. He stopped with the passenger door a step in front of me. I settled into the leather seat. "Let's get out of here."

"What about the drug?"

"I have enough in my backpack to take out an army. Swing by your place. Need to lock it down in the vault."

"What?!" Hanna screeched. "After what you just saw, you have the shit with you?"

Busted. She was hot, and I was cornered. "It's in the stable crystalline form, not the final serum." She wasn't appeased. I changed tactics. "We may need it to get Damon back. That is what you want, right?"

She pulled back on the psycho blonde, hesitating on her moral outrage. "Yes, that's all I want. As much as I may want to, we can't trade his life for hundreds of others. There has to be another way." She gripped my shoulder, leaning forward from the back seat. "I hired you, which makes me the boss. Find the other way."

"It will be safe in my vault," Ian assured her. "It isn't the first time the nuclear-grade vault will be used to bury secrets. Then we need to get back to Diamond's office. When I left, Dixon was cleaning up a video feed of a man identified as Damon."

I let my head rest, my eyes closed. "These asshats hunting for the raven, they have no clue what is going on. Someone is using them."

"They lost two of their teams. If they know it's you taking them out, if Trixie talks, we have a new problem. The name I got, Leo Krause, he's the left-hand man in a German nationalist group. The leader is a second-generation asshole named Karl Becker."

"Karl. Same name as the guy behind this evening's lab rats. Euro Rat went to school with him."

"You think these two are the ones who have Damon?" Hanna's emotions swung again. Now, fear was leading the band. She retreated, curling into the corner of the rear seat.

"Hey, wipe those tears," Ian said. "We're getting there. No, Becker and Krause don't have Damon or they wouldn't have sent in hired hands. We're looking for a competitor. A player who isn't in the game but should be. We'll find them. Trust us.

Try to get some rest."

Hanna nodded and sank deeper into the seat, the tension easing from her face. Apparently, she found comfort in Ian's words.

I don't know why. I didn't have a plan.

It took two and a half hours to get to Ian's building, make the safe deposit, then drive to my place. Hanna went to Dixon's apartment to shower. I could use one myself, but it had to wait. The reunion with Dix was sunshine and potato chips. That's when that other shoe, the one that hangs suspended over your head, dropped.

"It's Sam Irish. What the fuck is he doing with Damon? Play it again, Dix." I got up close and personal with the mega-sized screen mounted to my horsehair plaster wall. Back, forth, back, forth.

Ian swore, confirming the ID. "But...why?"

"Isn't that the question." I paced because I was hot. I knew he was playing me, but knowing someone is playing you and *knowing* someone is playing you are two completely different things. "What was he going to get out of sending Hanna to me to find a man he had?"

Dix spoke up from behind us. "I know where he's going. I'll tell you if you take me with you." I gave him a singular glare that foretold of pain and suffering. He cracked. "Edinburgh, Scotland. Can I go?"

"N—"

"Yes," Ian shouted over me. "Great idea. Go pack, I'll take care of the tickets."

With enough hooting and hollering to fill a square dance, Dixon was off. I glowered at Ian. He crossed his arms and stood his ground. Neither of us said a word until the back door closed.

"What the fuck? I won't have time to babysit Dix—"

"*He's* going to babysit *you*." Ian cut me off. Again. This was one habit that needed breaking with a wrecking ball. "You ready to talk about what was going on in that bathtub a few days ago? What Gabe's picture was doing in the bathroom? What that fucking letter was, turning your company over to me and Dix?"

"You found that?" I sort of forgot it existed.

"Yeah, I found that. Tidying everything up, saying your goodbyes. Jesus, Diamond, what the hell were you thinking?"

Since this whole thing started, I'd been too busy to think. His question brought it back in jarring black-and-white images.

There was no point to me. Every day was endless. I wasn't strong enough to outlast eternity.

I opened my mouth, but words didn't come.

"What happened to Gabe was criminal, and you made it right." Ian's voice was soft, just for me. "It didn't bring him back, I know, but lots of people lose their spouses to violence, and they don't kill themselves. You feel lost, I see it. But you're still in there. Until you find your way back, Dixon is with you. He loves you like, I don't know, a favorite aunt or an older sister. He's survived his father's fists, the system, juvie, but he won't survive your suicide. Don't give up on yourself. We're not."

My heart ached, like literally hurt inside my chest. "You don't play fair," I said, my voice a whisper.

"You're too important to play by the rules." He hugged me, and all the little pieces of me fell apart.

I pushed him away, but he didn't go. I was going to have a breakdown if I didn't get some space. "I'm all right. Really. We have work to do."

He stepped back, giving me room to breathe. "Let's get some plane tickets."

"I'm going to update Hanna. Something tells me you should buy three." For the first time, we had real direction. "Ian, add to your to-do list starting our own witness protection program. Damon and Hanna are our first customers." When he nodded, I left him to it and went to find my client. Across the cast iron landing were doors to the side-facing apartments. The one on this floor was filled with Five Finger Death Punch. I forewent the bedroom, thumping with bass that tested the structural integrity of my hundred-year-old building, searching for Hanna in the remaining eight hundred square feet. She was in the front room, sitting on a nice leather couch, her face in her hands. I came up behind her, startling her because she couldn't hear me call her name three times. Her face was damp, and it wasn't from the shower.

"Remember what I said?" I shouted at the top of my lungs. "Doubt doesn't play here."

Hanna dropped her head, hiding her tears beneath her hair. A few deep breaths and she was brave enough to face me. "I keep waiting for things to get better," she yelled. "Every time I think it can't get worse, it does. So much worse."

"We're at a turning point. Dixon tracked Damon to the airport, traveling with one of Britain's best agents. The good news is, he's not in the hands of terrorists. The better news is, you're going to get him back."

Cue kick-ass drum solo.

Twelve hours and twenty phone calls later, life was good (for the moment). I followed Dix up the narrow airplane aisle, smiling as he made friends with everyone around us. I'd spent too many hours in too many airports to find any of it amusing. Dixon was a dry sponge in a brand-new ocean. We settled in. Well, I settled. Dix played with everything. Tray table. Light. Air. Window shade. Seat belt. Seat back. Seat forward. Seat back. Seat forward.

Hanna sat in front of us. She wasn't talking to her seatmate. She'd said little since we left the building. She had grinned at Dix's reaction to everything airport-related. While the smile had been genuine, it was small compared to how much she worried. I reached around the seat and squeezed her shoulder. "No doubt. Remember."

She leaned into the aisle, turning so I could see her face. "No doubt," she said, but clearly did not believe.

The announcement called for our attention in preparation for take-off. Hanna would see. Once we were in Scotland and I found Irish, she would see reason to hope.

"Here we go!" Dixon watched out the window, bobbing his head to a backbeat only he could hear. The acceleration pushed us back in our seats. Then we were airborne. "Damn, look at all the houses. Didn't know there were so many. And look at the roads. Whoa, it just got foggy."

I glanced past him to the thick white veil. "We're in the clouds, Dix."

"Look at me, in the clouds." After admiring nature, he turned away from the window. Dixon plugged into his tablet and brought up a long list of movies. I had my own method of amusing myself. The next six hours gave me just enough time to figure out...

ONE HUNDRED WAYS TO KICK IRISH'S ASS

1. With my right foot
2. With my left foot
3. In stilettos
4. Wearing steel toe boots
5. Wearing elf shoes
6. Wearing snowshoes
7. Wearing cleats
8. With my knee
9. With my other knee
10. With Bruce Lee's knee
11. With a baseball bat
12. With a hockey stick
13. With a lacrosse stick
14. With a pool cue
15. At a swimming pool
16. Off a diving board
17. Off a cliff
18. Off a cliff with a bungee, so I could kick it again on the rebound
19. Off a skyscraper without a suicide net
20. Off a highway overpass at rush hour
21. In a tunnel, still at rush hour
22. In a cave filled with bats
23. At the center of the earth
24. At the other side of the earth, aka China
25. On the moon

26. On a rocket ship to the moon
27. On the command capsule falling back to the earth at terminal velocity
28. Without a parachute
29. With an umbrella, folded…and then expanded
30. With a selfie stick
31. With a riding crop
32. With silver spurs buffed until they shined like a star
33. On a horse
34. Behind a horse after a big meal
35. Under a horse, before the stall is cleaned
36. Tethered to a team of sled dogs, sans sled

(This is harder than I thought it would be.)

37. By a momma grizzly bear thinking he is threatening her babies
38. In a lumberjack competition where he's the pine log
39. Over the North Pole, while Santa isn't watching
40. Off a mountain
41. Across a glacier
42. Through thin ice
43. Off a bluff, only I'm not bluffing
44. In the middle of an ocean, any of them
45. Over a waterfall
46. Into a lake with water one degree above freezing
47. Into a boat lock, preferably empty
48. Off a ship in hostile waters
49. Off a bus on the wrong side of the tracks
50. Off an airplane over the Bermuda Triangle

(No, I don't want the chicken. We both know it's not really chicken.)

51. Eating a chicken pot pie
52. In a chicken coop filled with agoraphobic fowl
53. With tar and feathers
54. In a dog pound with big, vicious, slobbery canines

55. In the Cleveland Brown's Dawg Pound in December
56. In a hurricane
57. In a himacane
58. At high noon during a solar eclipse
59. With the pot of gold at the end of a rainbow
60. During Tropical Storm Diamond
61. On a tropical beach
62. In a desert sandstorm

(Having to get creative now. All the easy ones are taken.)

63. Indulging on the ultimate chocolate suicide dessert
64. With a flaming baked Alaskan
65. Sipping Café Brulot Diabolique imported from Antoine's in New Orleans
66. Tearing through the shrimp cocktail from St. Elmo's in Indianapolis
67. Using his body as a speedbump for Indy cars
68. Tying him to the tires on a NASCAR track
69. Using him as the finish line at Churchill Downs
70. With a horse whip sized for mammoths
71. Accompanied by five dozen beginner trumpet students
72. To the melody of a tone-deaf recorder choir
73. With the high step of the Ohio State University Marching Band's drum major
74. As target practice for Radio City Music Hall's Rockettes
75. Reenacting the William Tell apple story to the *William Tell Overture*

(How many more are there? Sheesh. I should have gone for fifty. It worked for shades of gray, but no, I had to set the bar high. Fucking bar.)

76. In a crushing hold to the bosom of a robust opera soprano during the signature aria
77. While shot from the cannon into a net gnawed on by Mothra

78. In the role of a traitor to a band of civil war reenactors
79. Amidst a fevered battle of LARPers with a wet noodle as his weapon
80. By defenestration through hurricane-grade glass
81. By castration with a—nope, that's taking things too far
82. By liquefaction in a sand pit with a swarm of biting ants
83. In a dunk booth by a major league pitcher with a gross of baseballs
84. As a target holder for a far-sighted knife thrower
85. Strung from a tree as the first-ever Irish piñata
86. To a serenade by a mariachi band lamenting his sad, pathetic life
87. Sober, totally sober. No alcohol, no caffeine, no sugar. Nothing
88. Tied to a kitchen chair while MaryAnn McNamara makes flaming shish kabobs
89. By an acupuncture school dropout using knitting needles

(Almost there. So...close...)

90. Using a nuclear-grade, exothermic reaction with him as the catalyst
91. By cryogenically freezing him and using his butt for a drum solo
92. Using a time machine to send him to fourteenth-century Europe when pretty much everything could kill you
93. Making him the center link in a three-way tug-of-war between Zeus, Poseidon, and Hades
94. Tying a dozen bags of gold to his body and pointing two dozen berserkers in his direction
95. Hog tying him with wax ropes and hanging him over an active volcano
96. With one leg tied behind his back in the running of

the bulls of Pamplona

97. By making him yell "Bingo" when he doesn't have bingo at the weekly game of the Anger Management Society
98. By getting a colonoscopy from a doctor with Parkinson's and without the benefit of muscle relaxants
99. By making him floss the teeth of a hundred, fire-breathing Irish dragons after gorging themselves on a peasant village

"Attention, passengers. We are about to start the final decent into Edinburgh. Please power off nonapproved devices and return tray tables and seat backs into their upright positions. Thank you."

100. By living with my mother for a month—wait, that's too cruel, even for him—for a week!

DEATH BY SELFIE STICK

Three needs dominated as I walked through the terminal at Edinburgh airport. One, get on the phone and tag the contacts who would find Irish in this haystack of a country. Two, find a clean, normal, water-driven toilet. I hate the closets they have the balls to call a bathroom on a plane. Three, get reintroduced to my favorite addiction, one that I walked away from under duress.

I was on the toilet, checking for messages, responding to the ones I'd sent out before boarding. Three loaded, including, surprise, one from Irish. At last, answers.

"Got your message about Hanna Lang," he said, shouting over background noise. "I would have handled her personally, but I'm covered for the time being. I looked into her enough to know she's legitimate." As his voice flowed thick and lilting, I saw his face and the half smile he wore when he was toying with a mark. "Her man was taken middle of the day, disappeared into thin air, so it seems."

I choked on his bullshit. "Only because that's how you wanted it to seem."

"He may have gone to California. Rumor is there's another woman."

"Bet you started the rumor."

"Hanna has need of your talents. You'll have to put your other plans on hold indefinitely."

I sat up straighter. "Other plans?" Did he know...he couldn't have...but then...

The toilet flushed.

"Son of a bitch!" Cold water splashed where cold water was just not welcome. I did the button and zipper thing and got out of the stall.

"Something wrong?" Hanna washed her hands, looking over her shoulder at me.

"I hate automatic flushers." I made with the soap and warm water. "Tell me again how you found O'Rourke?"

"I've already told you." She glanced around as she dried her hands, uncomfortable with the topic in our public location.

I pulled her into a handicap stall, blocking her exit.

"The dark web," she said quietly. "I did research and found the address to a message board for people who need special help. I posted a message, he responded."

"What did your message say?"

"Does it matter?"

"You're the psychologist. Is there anything that doesn't matter?"

She gave a little shake of her head. "I said my husband had been kidnapped from Calvert College and I wanted to hire someone to bring him home. No questions asked."

It was enough for Irish to recognize the man in question was the very one in his custody. "Then you met him? In person?"

"We messaged privately first. He asked questions about Damon, then he arranged to meet the next day. He said he couldn't help me, something about a previous engagement. He gave me your address and that ridiculous IOU."

"That's all?"

She exhaled heavily, her shoulders sagging. "He told me not to get my hopes up," she said in a soft voice. "The odds were not on my side."

Irish met with a woman who was connected to a man he snatched. He sent her my way, cashing in a marker worth a lot on the open market. Ten times as much on the black market. Why?

"Diamond?"

"Shhh. Don't interrupt." He told her not to expect to find him because he knew they were leaving the country. He left it to me to chase wild gooses, wasting her time and mine on a dead end. Was that his goal? To keep her busy? "What would you have done if O'Rourke walked away?"

"Gone back to the message board, I guess. O'Rourke was the first to answer not the only." She planted her hands on her hips. "It's O'Rourke, isn't it? You think he's playing some kind of game with me?"

Not with her, with me. The arrogant SOB would think I couldn't find him. Oh, yes. That was it. Irish set up this quest to keep Hanna busy, picking me as her witless guide.

I smiled. It was not friendly.

Hanna stepped back until she sat hard on the toilet. "You're scaring me."

"Those odds O'Rourke told you about? They just swung in your favor." I ripped the door open and stalked out, Hanna after me. Five women turned toward us. "What? Women don't go to the bathroom together in Scotland? It's the 2020s."

Hanna's soft laughter followed me out. "Two of them went in after us."

Dixon peered up from his place against the wall. "Hey, Diamond, what took you so long?" He unfolded his colt legs, rose, then leaned in close and dropped his voice. "I love how they talk here."

I paused, listening for the first time. The words floating in the air with vowels not heard at home. Accents on common words fell in uncommon places. Even laughter sounded somehow fancier. Imported. "Me, too. Come on, I'll introduce you to the real treasure of Scotland."

Into a store we paraded. There, proudly displayed on a bright red, yellow, and black display, was my favorite addiction. Walkers Shortbread cookies.

I took four. Five. Okay...six.

But they weren't all for me.

My phone chimed. "Here," I said, shoving money and the boxes of cookies into Dixon's hands. "Pay for these. It's Ian, I have to take this." I paced away, finding privacy in the cacophony of the airport terminal. "Hey. Any luck?"

"Two potentials. I'm getting pictures. Stay close."

"How about progress on this Karl and Leo?"

"Karl Becker just may be an evil genius. Multiple degrees in physics and mechanical engineering. He held low positions in government, which came to an abrupt end about the same time investigations were underway for bribery and sabotage. His father, Hans, started a pseudo-political party called the Danube Progressive Bewegung. It translates to Danube Progressive Movement. They have a website. Their mission is to preserve the German heritage for the next generation, including the countryside, language, and bloodlines. Hans was convicted of murdering four people who died during what he termed a protest demonstration at a restaurant in an immigrant neighborhood. He died in prison from pneumonia."

"Let me guess, Karl stepped into dear ol' dad's footprints?"

"Got it in one. Unlike his father, Karl isn't waving his arms for attention. The DPB is suspected behind bomb threats, broken windows, and vandalism, but no charges have been filed. I found three manifestos published by Karl both on the internet and in media. His older writing was tame compared to the recent one. It seems Karl is taking the refugee crisis from the Syrian civil war personally. Diamond, I'm no psychiatrist, but he's escalating. He's calling for a cataclysmic retaking of Germany."

"And he wants the Raven serum Damon and his pals concocted. Gee, I wonder what for? Dig up anything on Leo?"

"Leo Krause is Karl's muscle. He grew up on the wrong side of the tracks in Berlin, in and out of police custody for fighting and stealing. All small-time stuff. Leo went to live with Hans and Karl when he was thirteen. When Karl left for university,

Leo went with him, working as a janitor's assistant."

"It was just Hans and the two boys for all those years."

"Hans was married. They had two children. When they split, she took the daughter with her. He didn't remarry."

My gears were in motion, grinding through the fog of the transatlantic flight. "This is good. We know who is behind the scavenger hunt for Raven, who killed the first two scientists. Are Jeremy Hardy and China Whiting secure?"

"Yes. Jeremy and Napoleon are in Upstate New York. Our California friends got to China fifteen minutes after Karl's hires. Hear she's hell on wheels with mace. She's tucked away."

"Good. Two less tools for Karl's merry band of bastards to use against us. Irish returned my call, leaving a message with so much bullshit the grass around his ass-kicker boots had to be three feet tall. He met with Hanna, knowing he was sitting on Damon."

"Why?"

"Isn't that the question? My guess, he wanted her quiet and out of the way. He sets her on me, expecting I'll hold her hand to find the fiancé that isn't missing." I turned, facing out the oversized window to the concrete tarmac inches away. "He doesn't think I can find him."

"No, he doesn't think you'll figure out that you should find him."

"He's underestimating me. Again. And you and Dixon." Suddenly, I felt predatory. "Maybe I should give him a taste of the serum I'm not smart enough to find."

Ian chuckled. He never failed to be amused by Irish ending up on the losing end of a proposition. "Wait. You didn't bring some of it with you, did you?"

"Now, do you really think I would take a lethal concoction onto a commercial flight when I'm going to be sitting next to a seventeen-year-old jackrabbit?"

"Right. Good." Quiet dropped in for a moment. "How did the kid do on his first flight?"

And we got to the real reason for his call coming fifteen

minutes after the wheels touched down. I laughed. "Fine. After the thrill of takeoff, he plugged into his tablet. I kept telling him to sleep. When I woke up, he was halfway through another movie. He's gonna crash hard at some point."

"Heads-up, he was scheming to get you to let him drive."

"Oh, that's not happening. He can barely drive on the right side of the road. I can only imagine the carnage with him driving on the wrong side."

We signed off when Ian had another call come in. I listened to my other messages. One was from Trixie of the Cleaning Ladies, inviting me to meet her for coffee. She promised me an offer I couldn't refuse. As far as potential employers go, Trixie was cream of the crop. But I wasn't looking to become anyone's employee.

The aggrieved Lieutenant Trevor at Calvert College left a message. Despite the chemistry department resembling crème brûlée, there had been another break-in. His contact at the local police department told him Damon's house had been targeted two more times. They were taking appropriate measures.

I looked up in time to see Hanna horse-collar Dixon, using his hoodie to stop him from following an older man in a kilt.

"Good news, I hope," Hanna said as they crossed the sea of people. She held out the bag, from which I took a box of cookies.

"Mostly." I ripped open the cardboard and the plastic liner inside. A decadent, golden nugget went into my mouth. I melted along with the buttery goodness. "God, I love these." I offered them to Dix and Hanna. "We're closing in on Irish and Damon."

"Who's Irish?" Hanna asked. "These are good. I can't believe I haven't had them before."

"He's the guy who sent you to Diamond," Dixon said. "There's no frosting."

"When cookies are this good, all frosting can do is fuck it up." And I went for another. "It's been too long."

"The guy I met was named O'Rourke."

"Not his real name. None of them use their real names,"

Dixon explained as he dug into the box.

Hanna was uncomfortable with the idea. "Your name isn't Andrew Dixon?"

"Mine is. I'm like in training. Someday, I'm going to have another name. I have some ideas."

We started walking again, out of the airport and into a cab. Dixon regaled us with the lo-ong list of potential names, most of which sounded like they belonged in 1970s porn. Longbow Johnson. Cockand Hammer.

One minute, I was in a cab, enjoying the ride to our hotel. The next minute, I had one hundred eighty pounds of man-child in my lap.

"It's a castle, Diamond! It's a fucking castle!"

Out my window was the very impressive sight of Edinburgh Castle.

"Look at it! How do you get up there? How did they build it on the side of a mountain? Do you think they threw people over the sides?" Question after question. From the quizzical to the practical to the fantastical. Then he shifted back onto his side of the seat and grabbed my shoulders. "Can we go?"

In that moment, I knew exactly what he looked like when he was five years old.

Hanna chuckled softly. "It is impressive. Too bad we aren't tourists."

"Macousin keeps the peace. Ayekin getchuin places those bedamned tearboose people can note go." This came from our driver, who watched Dixon in the mirror more than he looked out the windshield.

"You can?!" Dixon wasn't giving up on the exclamation points anytime soon. And how he understood the thick accent was a puzzle to me. But then, it wasn't the first time Dixon's ear made sense of what sounded like gibberish. "Diamond! He can get us in places tour bus people can't go! How freaking great is that?!"

Tour bus people. Yeah, that's what I heard.

"Maybe—"

"Which means yes!" Dixon leaned between the seats, flashing his stunning smile. "Hook us up, Jack."

"Aye, laddie. Here you are," the driver said, double-parking in the middle of a stone building that took up the block. Every thirty feet or so, a set of stairs led up to a door. The door in front of us had a small, tasteful sign indicating we had arrived at The Chester Residence. I paid the driver, leaving Dixon to make arrangements for the castle. Hanna and I checked in. Our room wasn't in this building but the one abutting it. Hanna and I walked with the woman from the front desk, talking about the beauty of the street, of the stone facing, of the colorful doors. We made two lefts and found the cab with Dixon and our bags idling in front of a subtle, distinguished plaque announcing our destination. This entrance was quieter and more discreet, and it suited me perfectly.

Our room was an apartment on the third floor.

The only apartment on the third floor.

A master bedroom—damn right, it was mine—a second bedroom with two beds, a comfortable living room, and full bathroom and kitchen were ours. Our hostess walked through, explaining how the doors to the rooms needed to be kept closed for fire safety. Our eyes connected, and I knew that she knew that wouldn't be happening. She explained the keys and the televisions and the Wi-Fi before she left us.

"Dixon, you're on the couch," I said, noticing Hanna looked uncomfortable at the idea of sharing a room with him.

"'K. What's in the kitchen?" He disappeared behind a heavy door.

"He's doomed to disappointment," I said. "Fair warning, we will have to hit a grocery store or we're in danger of him turning on us."

"We can't have that." She chuckled softly again before sobering. "How long do you think we'll be here?"

"We're booked in for five days, but this is going to happen

quick. I can feel it. Tomorrow. Day after at the most."

"I'm out of my mind with worry. Damon, he's not a hard man, you know?" She took a deep breath. "O'Rourke, you called him Irish, you think he kidnapped Damon? Is he the one you said was one of Britain's best agents?"

I knew the hard questions were coming. Truth was, I hadn't figured out all the answers. Did I trust Irish? Yes. Totally. Unequivocally. I gave her the only thing I could. "He's one of the good guys."

She dropped her head, shook it slowly. When she lifted it, her blue eyes flashed with something hard and sharp. It was just for a moment, but it was there. She turned away from me, toward her bedroom. "Good guys can be monsters, too."

We spent the rest of the day masquerading as tourists. We fed Dix at a pub, walked him along the Royal Mile, took him to a grocery store where we bought enough for a week. We napped, ate again.

Midnight came. This far north, this close to the summer solstice, the sky was stuck at twilight. I took the last cookie from the third package, ate it with my coffee. The moon hung over the rooftops, seeing everything, knowing everything.

A text notification made me look down. It was Ian's contact. I called the phone number. "This is Diamond."

"Bennie. I have the photos you asked for. When can we meet?"

"Edinburgh Castle, tomorrow, two o'clock. The Scottish Crown Jewels."

'CAUSE WHERE ELSE WOULD YOU FIND A DIAMOND?

The sun shone down warmly as we hiked up Castle Hill, chasing away the nip in the air. Dixon paced along the spiraling wall, his fingers in constant contact with God knew what. It was his first castle, and he seemed determined to experience every part of it. Hanna walked between me and Dix. She had been quiet this morning, cooking breakfast for us. Even when Dixon declared her the world's best breakfast maker, she had been subdued. Nerves did that to some people.

Me, I get loud.

"Why couldn't they just text you the address?" she asked. "Or told it to you."

Dixon snorted. "Nothing digital is secure. Look at what I did with the security footage. Tapping into lines isn't that hard either."

"He's right," I said. "And we want everyone else to keep guessing. I have an idea of where we're going, but I want confirmation."

Hanna stopped in her tracks. "You know where Damon is?"

"I suspect. We'll know in two hours." We rounded a corner and were welcomed by an ancient entry. I never failed to get a small rush of awe in places that predate my experience by a hundred decades. How many feet crossed this threshold before mine? How many felt this same type of amazement? How many felt abject fear knowing they wouldn't be leaving on their own two feet?

We used our gifted tickets and continued into a large, open courtyard. Dixon slowed down. He was messaging. Moving at now glacial speed, he was fodder for a herd of tourists plowing across the courtyard. The group of fifty-some people were crowded together, walking in an offensive formation that ensured they stayed together, got where they were going, and weren't infiltrated.

Hanna hit Dixon from the side, her arms coming up to carry him with her.

"Hey," he shouted as his body lurched perpendicular to his direction. "I was..." he trailed off as he caught sight of the pack and heard the distinctly Asian banter. His lips grew into a wide smile as he looked down at the people. Everyone was shorter than him.

"You need to pay attention," Hanna scolded. "We have those same hordes in Germany. They stop for no one. Who are you texting?"

"Mac. Jack told me to text him when we were here. Hey, he's texting back. Sweet, he says to meet him at the argle battery, whatever that is."

Hanna tipped the screen her way. "Argyle Battery. Let's look at the map. On the right, past the visitor information."

"Sweet. Come on." Dix kicked it into third gear, leaving us behind.

Hanna looked between us, then jogged to catch up with the longer legged teen.

I was not running.

Mac the Scotsman was as rugged and welcoming as the country that bore him. Little flecks of color remained in his white beard, remnants of the red that was once abundant. He clapped Dixon on the back hard enough to make the kid stagger forward. Hanna was shaking Mac's hand as Dixon waved me closer. “Come here, Diamond. Meet Mac.”

He measured me with an eye sharper than the façade implied. “Diamond, is it?”

“Tara Dixon. I’m his older sister.” That was the name on my passport. This time. “Diamond is a family nickname.”

“True? And what be your nickname, boy?” Mac’s bushy brows lifted and pressed, offering color commentary to what came out the mouth.

“Talc,” I said, cutting Dixon off. “He had nappy rash issues as a boy.”

“Diamond!” Dixon squealed my name as Mac rolled with laughter.

“Take cover!” The bloody Scotsman bellowed suddenly.

I shoved Hanna and Dixon into the wall, shielding them with my body. Mac leapt in front of me, waving at an approaching pack of tourists as if they were pigeons. “Over with you. Over with you and your fecking phones.” He stood his ground with me beside him, becoming immovable objects forcing the thick column to morph around us. “Fecking bus tours. Good for business, bad for me constitution. Let’s be off. I’m on my break. It’s enough time to tell a story or two not fit for printing in the pansy pamphlet.”

Dixon was Mac the Scot’s shadow through the castle. He hung on every word as tales of victory and defeat, betrayal and retribution were spun. He asked questions and, little by little, his Washington, D.C. accent took on the Scot’s lilt. Hanna and I followed. I kept my attention on the crowd. The walkways and rooms were tightly packed with accents from around the world. In the close confines, it would be easy to plant a knife in a kidney and disappear. Hanna was torn between keeping up with Dixon and being with me. She knew I was meeting someone, but I hadn’t shared the details. She asked, but when I deflected, she didn’t press. I knew it was hard on her, but this wasn’t her world. Ian’s contact was a friend-of-a-friend type of deal. Protecting his identity was paramount. This was not happy hour with the boys.

As the time approached two, I made an excuse and left the group. Hanna tried to come with me, but I made it clear she was to stay. This was a solo operation.

I leaned against a bench outside the building housing The Honours of Scotland, the Scottish Crown Jewels. I studied the crowd, snacking on a personal-size package of Walkers shortbreads. Bennie would be wearing the Loch Ness monster.

Two o'clock on the dot, a small pixie of a woman hiked my way. She wore a T-shirt with the Loch Ness monster, Big Foot, and Santa Claus over the words "I Believe." Her short hair was a baby blue and twisted into spikes around her head. Her eyes were dark, her lips a darker shade of blue. Behind her were two gangly men. Both wore spikes in their hair and around their throats. They faded into the background, allowing the woman to approach alone. She came directly to the bench, dropped her backpack on the seat, and sat. "Do you have the time?"

It was the right opening line. "It's five o'clock somewhere," I said, "but here, it's two. Have you seen the jewels before?"

"Yes, many times. I'm partial to diamonds. Care to have a look?" Bennie rose, shouldering her bag. We went into the building, walking past security working crowd control. The congested space contained a bus horde and three families who had the unfortunate timing to be caught in with them. One father stood behind the group, his daughter on his shoulders to see over the four-deep line. A mother was as close to the glass as was legal, sheltering a boy of ten or so.

Employing a groupthink that sociologists would soon be studying, the horde turned their backs on the jewels, raising phones of all sizes and colors to snap selfies. Lines shifted with those in the back exchanging positions with those in the front. The boy cried out when his mother was shoved.

"Mind holding my map?" Bennie held one of the standard-issue maps to me. "Me shoe needs tying."

"You live dangerously," I said, eyeing the band of bastard bus tourists who'd pummel the pixie without noticing. I opened the map under the guise of reading it. What I actually studied was a high-resolution image of Sam Irish. He owned four properties in the UK, each very different. Ultra-urban, sedate suburban, gritty industrial, and the one where this photo was taken, rugged countryside. The gritty industrial, situated in Edinburgh's underbelly, had been my first choice. It was defensible, nearly impenetrable, and nearby other resources. Instead, he'd chosen the small town in the Highlands. It was secluded, defensible, and invisible.

The photos were taken with a telephoto lens. Irish was in all of them, wearing his no-bullshit working face. He was point in a three-person parade. Damon was the chocolate filling between vanilla wafers. The bottom cookie had the unmistakable profile of Russia's answer to Sam Irish. Yuri Popov.

Americans. Brits. Germans. Now Russians.

Damon was up to his neck. We had at least three governments colluding to make a scientist disappear. This confirmed it. When this was over, there was no going home for Hanna and Damon, no picking up life as it was.

I wasn't worried anymore about Damon's life, in the heartbeat sense. Irish and Popov were two of the best. If they'd wanted Damon dead, the deed would have been done. If they wanted him alive, likely it was for what was in his head. Since I had in hand what Damon had in the bush, so to speak, I had leverage.

Adding an envelope with payment, I refolded the map. Bennie's cue to stand. She took the map and photos back. "Thank you."

The room was packed tightly, the flow of people made it a one-way road. With business concluded, Bennie regaled me with the history of the jewels we were admiring.

I wanted out. Short and simple.

I sucked it up, putting on the face of an interested visitor while I continuously scanned the crowd. Behind me was a man who moved with the crowd but didn't once look at the glimmering display.

Rookie mistake.

I pointed to a scepter that would have made one hell of a weapon if I could have gotten my hands on it. "We need to exit. Now."

Bennie looked to where I pointed. "Trouble?"

"Tall, blond, and obviously staring at us."

She glanced over my shoulder, then snorted. "One minute." She texted quickly, her thumbs flying over the digital letters. We stepped forward as the response loaded. "There are two outside. Either side of the door."

"This ought to be fun." In the glass reflection, I saw that Bennie wore the same expression.

"We need to get out first. Follow me." She used shoulders and elbows to infiltrate the heart of the Asian tourist horde in front of us. A scarf dangling from a purse became mine. I pushed it into Bennie's hand, and her distinct blue hair disappeared. I had to walk with my knees bent, bringing me down to average height.

The middle-aged women next to me frowned.

"*Konnichiwa*," I said with a smile. It was not returned. "*Ni hao*." Nada. I was about to break out my limited knowledge of Korean when Tall, Blond, and Obvious made his move. He slid along the back wall, coming around our flank. The front of our horde was already at the door. We would be out in under twenty seconds. TBO was even with us, he was tracking me, his gaze then darting for Bennie. She'd disappeared. She'd pushed ahead, putting four people between us, blending like a chameleon. The horde necked as it morphed to fit through the doorway. TBO was stuck in the eddy at the inside corner of the door, the crowd rebuffing his entrance.

Outside, the sunlight was blinding. Two men were standing on either side of the door, not so tall but equally blond and obvious. They looked like they were about to commit assault. A few more steps with our horde camouflage and I rose to my full height, my quads burning from the ruse. Bennie's goth friends were loitering at the bench, arguing over a sandwich. Or that was what it was supposed to look like. As soon as they made their partner, the pair jumped to their feet, shoving each other, shouting. They danced in a circle, the horde gave way, making room for the violent actions and harsh words. Green Goth shoved Purple Goth backwards. Hard. Purple Goth went into TBO3. TBO2 drove across the crowd. He grabbed Purple by the forearm and swung him off his partner.

Green caught his friend, then got in TBO2's face. "Keep your fecking hands to yourself, you fecking asshole."

"You filthy animals better mind your place." TBO2's German accent sealed it. We had contact with the other side.

Then it was two-on-two in an all-out color showdown. While the skirmish raged, the original TBO shot around the outside of the fleeing horde. His target was Bennie, who stood off to the side, the scarf around her shoulders. With a sea of people between us, I could only watch as TBO hit Bennie hard, tackling her to the ground, her head bouncing off the cobblestone. Her boneless body laid where it fell as TBO stripped the backpack from her shoulder and ran.

Without thought, I chased. The cobblestone road sloped downward sharply enough that footing mattered. TBO slipped the backpack on and ran like the devil was chasing him. And I was. He rushed through people, shoving them into my path. Steadily, I closed the gap, ducking and dodging most, catching a kid he literally threw at me. TBO took the first right, running up the few steps and then charging through people littering the long approach to a chapel. Afraid of losing him inside the building, I kicked it up a gear. I stopped inside the threshold to get the lay of the space.

And I started laughing.

TBO paced along the very solid wall at the other end of the chapel. One way in. Same way out.

He turned when he heard me. His eyes went flat, his jaw squared. Whatever idea spawned in his head was a bad one. An elderly woman wandered close, oblivious to the danger. She squealed as TBO spun her, her back to his chest, a vicious knife pressed to the folds of her neck.

"Mum? MUM!" A middle-aged woman lunged forward.

"Stay back. Back or I'll kill her." He drew the knife in a slow, deliberate show of intent. Blood welled in the thin line. The elderly woman panted in a high-pitched whine, stepping in the direction the man behind her wanted. Her short legs couldn't keep up with his long-legged strides. She stumbled repeatedly, held up only by the arm now wrapped under her breasts. The gathered compressed, making way for the kidnapper and his hostage to pass. At the doorway, she tripped on his feet, collapsing like a house of cards. TBO let her fall. His free hand caught her hair, pulled. "Get up, you cow. Now."

I took two running steps and hit TBO solidly in the shoulder. The woman's scream mixed with TBO's harsh curses. We fell in a pile. He didn't let go of the woman. He laid below me on his side, knife hand on top. I fought to get the backpack off one of his shoulders. A white-hot burn told me his knife had found muscle. Twice. I leapt off, ready for a fight. TBO let the old woman go, focusing on me.

He swung the knife in a wide, crazed, horizontal arc. I leapt backward. He swung again. I leapt again, putting me in the front line of the audience. The mostly female crowd gasped and shrieked, racing away from me. A wall was at my back. Three feet high. Maybe three and a half. It was jumpable, but who the fuck knew what was below and how far down. I couldn't see.

"You're mine, bitch."

"In your dreams, loverboy." I snatched a thin, metal wand from a retreating woman, holding it overhead as TBO bore down at me. The selfie stick bent, the plastic end snapped off, giving me up without so much as a sorry. Still, it was enough to deflect the blow and give me the moment I needed to retaliate. I pressed forward, creating space to work. He had the advantages of height, weight, and reach.

Me? I was meaner.

He came at me again, telegraphing his over-the-shoulder

swing. I blocked it and buried the jagged edge of the selfie stick in his soft belly. He shouted in surprise as much as pain, his weight coming down over me. With a lowered shoulder, I let his momentum take me back. Then I used it against him, lifting him enough that gravity carried him over the wall.

The crowd screamed.

The body landed.

Game over.

I looked over the wall. TBO's body laid across the headstones of a small cemetery, the selfie stick protruding from his belly, his neck broken. And he was still wearing Bennie's backpack.

Fuck. I hope she didn't have anything illegal in it.

I turned back to the crowd. Dozens of wide eyes stared with a mix of intrigue and horror, waiting to see what I would do next. I swiped another selfie stick, broke it over my knee, and tossed it at the owner's feet. "No selfie sticks!"

As heads tucked together, quiet murmurs were exchanged, and the damned selfie sticks were stowed. I nodded, satisfied something good had come out of this mess. My name was shouted like a command, and the sea of people biblically parted. Dixon ran up the middle, Hanna on his heels. Dix didn't stop, running into me and planting us both into the ancient chapel wall. "He almost killed you."

"Not even close." I thumped his shoulder, pushing back on the emotion that swamped him. "I'm the same badass I always was. I'm gonna kick Ian's butt for talking shit behind my back."

He let me go, awkwardly. "Don't get me in trouble or he won't let me drive."

Hanna gasped beside us, getting our attention. All the color had drained out of her face as she stared at the scene below. She'd gone from German pale to Casper white. "Did...did he say anything?"

"Said he wanted to make me his bitch. I declined."

Whistles cut through the crowd's murmurs. The calvary was coming. What felt like forever was only a few minutes. "Get

Hanna to a bench before she passes out." Some people just don't have the constitution for the messy parts of this business. Uniformed guards flooded the area. Looked like I was going to find out how good the cover Ian created was.

"On your knees. Hands where I can see them."

Yeah, like I hadn't heard that line before.

EVERY SIXTY SECONDS, A MINUTE PASSES IN THE HIGHLANDS

"Not her. She's one of the good guys." Bennie had an ice pack pressed to her head and her own Scottish escorts at either elbow. The two guards led her to the front of our little scene. "She went after the man who attacked me and stole my bag." The blue-haired pixie came to my defense, towering over me as I knelt on the cobblestones.

"She saved my life." The former hostage pushed away from her daughter to wrap a claiming arm around my shoulder. Her chin was up, challenging authority. "She's a hero."

Yeah, I liked the way that sounded.

"A hero, is she?" The guy with the disbelieving intonation wore a name tag that read J. Stewart and a mustache worthy of a hall of fame.

"She pinned that animal to the ground until I could pull my mother away. She's more than a hero," the daughter said, "she's a…she's a.."

Wait for it…

"…a heroine."

Ah. Well. I could work with that. Yeah. I could work with that. A hero elevated to the *ine*th-degree.

"He stabbed her. Twice." Daughter pointed to the meaty part of my thigh. It didn't look like much. My black pants had two neat slits cut. The material was soaked, but black plus red equaled black, so there was little to see. Feel was a different story. Crisis over, I felt the fire licking my leg as it worked overtime to hold me upright.

Stewart raised a bushy brow. "And where be this man?"

Sixty people pointed to the empty space over the wall.

Stewart walked past me and leaned over the wall. He didn't gasp or smirk, he didn't raise a finger or an eyebrow. He simply said, "I see," as if German criminals with broken necks and sporting selfie sticks were a daily occurrence. Returning to me, he offered a hand to help me up. "Let's get you looked at and we'll get statements."

And that was how we got to see the working side of Edinburgh Castle. It wasn't all bad. I was stitched up, given a shot of antibiotics along with a bill that would go on my client's expense sheet. Bennie's bag was returned, intact and unsearched. Dixon got to spend more time with his buddy, Mac, who turned out to be a senior officer with the Castle's security.

Dead guy turned out to be exactly that. No wallet, no credit cards, no ID. After several rounds of *I saw the man tackle the young woman and take her bag, so I chased him and then he ran into the chapel and took the older lady hostage and so I tackled him and that's when he stabbed me, so I rolled off him and he charged me and I grabbed what was handy and defended myself*, I signed my name—well, not *my* name—on the solid black line and was generously given a ride down the thigh-killing hill.

Back at The Chester Residence, I climbed the stairs as normally as possible, holding my breath to avoid groaning. Dixon was watching. After redressing the wound and cleaning myself up, I logged onto the internet and made arrangements for the next leg of our quest. For what came after, I needed Dixon. He was in the living room, aka his bedroom, lying on his back, watching videos and finishing off a box of Walkers.

"You ready to work?" I straddled the arm of the couch, the height easy on my leg.

"Sure." He sat up, and crumbs rained to the cushion. "What are we doing?"

"Work with Ian. I want to connect with someone. Karl, Leo, their UK affiliates. Don't care as long as they can negotiate for a purchase. A large purchase."

He pulled his laptop to the coffee table and made with his lightning-fast fingers. "What are we buying?"

"We're selling. Poe's Raven. Let's take these asswipes for a crisp five million."

"Coolio. I'll scream for you when I have something."

"Calling works. No need for screaming. This is a nice neighborhood." I gave him my troublemaker smile, just for fun. "Well, it was until we moved in."

I left him laughing and went to Hanna's door. A two-finger rap warned her of my entrance. She stood at the window overlooking the early evening street. She turned away quickly but not before I caught her crying. "Problem? I mean, any new ones?"

She chuckled softly, but it didn't penetrate her sadness. "No, just the old ones. I really hoped today you would find out where Damon is and tomorrow I'd have him back. It was foolish, I know. Still, I never dreamed things would go as badly as they did today. You were stabbed. My God, you killed a man. And we got nothing." She shook her head, turning away from me, back to the window. "Damon is still as lost to me as if he were on the moon."

"We're close," I said quietly, my hand going to her shoulder. "Tomorrow, we'll be closer."

"But...but how?"

"I got the information. The question is, how did the TBOs know we would be there?" It was a question I hadn't had time to think through before.

"TBOs?"

"Tall, Blond, and Obvious. The dead one followed me into the Crown Jewels. The two that ran like rats from a ship waited outside. Bennie's friends distracted them. They were tracking me. They didn't know who she was until I walked in with her."

"But...that doesn't make sense." She pressed her palm to her head as if it ached.

"They were tipped off." I paced as I ticked off the people who knew. Dixon, Hanna, and me. Ian. Jack the cab driver and his brother, Mac the Scot. "Did you mention it to anyone here at the hotel?"

"I...well, yes. Remember we talked about the castle with the woman who showed us to our rooms. And Dixon told the waiter last night."

"Dixon told anyone who would listen. Fuck. I'll bet a dozen people knew where we were headed today. And when."

Hanna stepped into my path, her hands set lightly on my arms. It wasn't a threatening position, but I stepped back, away from the contact. "For Dixon," she said, "this is like a fantasy. Bigger. Coming here was beyond anything he could imagine. You know my field is traumatized youths. From the first night I stayed in his rooms, I knew what he was. I don't need to know the details to know, in some ways, he has grown up knowing more of the world than anyone should and, in other ways, his world has been very small. He told me the farthest from home he'd ever been was a field trip to the Smithsonian zoo. In one day, you shattered the record, taking him to a place of wonderful accents and cookies and castles. A place he literally was incapable of imagining."

I heard the truth in her insanely calm, professional voice. "You're right, this is a big deal for Dix, but what's your point?"

"Don't go too hard on him. *If* he did give away 'our position,' he did it because he was happy. I don't think he's had a lot of reason to be happy."

I wasn't mad at Dixon. One, while I may consider Hanna's field more art than science, she was right about him. Two, he wasn't just a kid, he was mine. Three, it's easier to stay mad at a puppy than Andrew Dixon. I wouldn't go too hard on him, ever, but I didn't respond to her analysis of Dixon; it was private.

"We're leaving first thing in the morning."

She gasped. "Where are we going?"

"A little town on the southern shore of the fabled Loch Ness. Maybe we'll get lucky and catch a monster of our own."

The following morning, Dixon challenged the notion that I wouldn't get mad at him when every fifteen minutes for over three hours he nagged me to let him drive.

"Diamond, can I drive?"

"No." Clean. Simple. Definitive. End of story.

"Come on," he said with so much whine in his voice, I wished I had cheese to stuff in his mouth. "I've driven on the wrong side of the road before."

I looked into his dark eyes. "Exactly."

"I mean on purpose."

"Exactly."

Then he'd settle into the back seat. Plotting. Strategizing.

"Diamond, you're looking tired. I can take a turn."

"No."

"The National Highway Traffic Safety Administration estimates drowsy driving was responsible for seventy-two thousand crashes, forty-four thousand injuries, and eight hundred deaths in 2013. It's real, Diamond. They made an infographic. It's probably higher here because you fuck up and you fall off a mountain."

So hard not to laugh. "What's the statistic on annoying passengers being thrown out of windows?"

"Defenestration? I'll look it up."

I did a double take. "How do you know that word?"

"Remember Toto, from school? It was his favorite word for a while. If you're going to defenestrate me, you're going to have to take your hands off the wheel. And if you're going to take your hands off the wheel, I might as well drive."

"No." But he kept going. Dix earned points for creativity and, I'll woman up and admit, he kept me from getting drowsy.

"Whoa. It's a freaking gated community." Dixon leaned

between me and Hanna, gawking at our destination. The gate opened and we rolled through the tree-dotted grounds, following the twisting road until we reached the parking area and the sprawling, gothic building. "You got us a castle of our own!"

"Not the whole thing," I said, unable to hold in my laughter. "Just an apartment for a few days. I didn't have a lot of choice, booking at the last minute." I climbed out of the car, my leg punishing me for the hours in the same position. Maybe I should have let Hanna drive.

"Welcome to The Highland Club," a big voice boomed. "Just arrived? Registration is through this door."

We were escorted to our room via a facility tour. It was a good thing Dixon wore a hoodie. I used it to save his face from planting into eighteenth-century walls as he looked everywhere but where his feet were going. Not unjustifiably. This iconic building began life as an English fortification in 1729 and later became St. Benedict's Abbey. The walls were stone with tall, arched windows, the floors mosaic tiles. Statues dotted the hallways, and figures and shapes were cast into pillars.

The only monks in residence were those in the cemetery. The Highland Club now provided permanent and temporary housing of various sizes, including ours. The penthouse.

What the hell. It's only money.

I left setting up shop to Hanna and Dixon, donned a red wig, and went out to reacquaint myself with the charming town of Fort Augustus. I'd been here twice, both times with Irish, using the cottage he kept in The Highland Club for some well-earned rest and relaxation. On the south end of Loch Ness, Fort Augustus had come to define Scotland for me. Kind and generous people. Tough, gorgeous landscape. And green. Every shade of green imaginable.

It had been five years since my last visit. Not a lot had changed. Some storefronts had new signs. The bridge over the canal still spun to allow boats to move to and from Loch Ness. The bridge over River Oich hadn't moved and was still a great place to admire nature. The store too small to be called a grocery by our standards still managed to have at least one of everything I wanted.

Grocery bags dangled from my wrists as I toured the parking areas around the main Abbey building. The white Audi in Bennie's photos was parked outside Irish's cottage, keeping a blue BMW company. I continued along, just a tourist, picking up some staples, should anyone be looking. Eventually, I came to a door and used my key to enter. No one watching would know I was on the opposite end of the building from our apartment.

I could walk up to the cottage, knock on the door, trust the muscle inside wouldn't shoot me on the spot, and ask Irish what the hell was going on. But fuck him. He'd made me play a game. I'd make him play one, too.

First, I'd make him go to The Boathouse, a small restaurant on the grounds with good food and great memories. Then I'd make him go to the grocery store and buy me more Walkers. Then, I'd have him go to The Moorings, a restaurant on the other side of the canal that was our favorite for takeout. That's when I'd make my move.

I unlocked our door and pushed it open. "Dix! Got food." His size thirteens echoed on the hard floor, sounding as if a half-dozen teens were charging my way. "Is your computer up and running?"

"Yeah, what do you need?"

"How do you say, 'We need to talk. Six o'clock. The Boathouse. Don't make me come get you' in Gaelic?"

I was in The Boathouse at six o'clock when Sam Irish came through the door. I sat at a table with a glass of wine and a book. The hair of my black wig fell around my face, hiding everything but the oversized glasses perched on my nose. He saw me. He dismissed me when the host greeted him. "Do you have a reservation, sir?"

"I'm meeting someone."

"Their name?" When Irish didn't answer, the host filled in

the blank. "We are booked until nine tonight. With the name, I can show you to a table."

Irish turned the reservation book, skimming the names. "No. It's none of those."

"You wouldn't be Mr. O'Rourke, would you?"

Irish froze. Not a single muscle twitched. I surprised him with the name. "If I am?"

"I have a message for you." The host earned his hundred euros. "A young man came in just after we opened. I told him, as I told you, we are booked tonight. He explained he arranged to meet you here but couldn't wait and asked me to give this to you."

"Thank you." Irish accepted the envelope, turned away from the host, and opened it.

I watched him through my faux bangs, squeezing my tender leg to keep a smile from my face. I read his lips. The language he was using would make Google translate blush.

He turned on the host aggressively. "Are you sure it was a man?"

"Yes," he said, then hesitated. "I thought so, at least, but these days, you can't be sure without a peek under the kilt."

I stayed where I was, sipping my wine, turning my pages for four minutes. I left money for the bill and stopped at the host stand. "Thank you for playing along."

"What was in the envelope, if you don't mind me asking?"

"My grocery list." I tipped the host a twenty. It was an American thing to do, but the guy had earned it. I walked at a leisurely place to my final destination. Yuri Popov was likely covering Irish, but the expert marksman was a fish out of water until he had a location and a target. The location was on the back of a very special bottle of scotch.

I sat at a picnic table, my hair now red, with a local who liked to hear himself talk as much as I did. Putting my discipline to practice, I did not check the time every two minutes, calculating when Irish would come stalking my way. I kept tabs on all who came and went. None fit the mold of Popov, the ugliest man I'd ever met. He would go for a vantage point. His choices were intentionally limited.

Finally, Irish appeared. He prowled down the street like he'd chew up and spit out any car stupid enough to get in his way.

"And that's when I shot the lying dog!" My companion roared with laughter. I joined in, changing my pitch. His laughter subsided. He used his napkin to mop up his tears. "Me wife nearly killed me. Turns out, she was fond of that particular brother. Speaking of brothers..."

His monologue provided the perfect cover. He was loud and brash and everyone looked our way. Irish saw me, but then he didn't see me. He saw a couple when he was hunting a single. Once Irish gave up on us, I went into the restaurant, using the bathroom to shed my wig and my plus-one. I stepped into the evening sun to find Irish planted in the middle of the sidewalk, staring intently across the canal.

This was one of those moments that made for an awesome line. I had five steps to figure one out.

What's a guy like you doing in a nice town like this? No. Boring.

Leave the haggis, take the cannoli. Uh-huh.

I poked my fingers in his back, "Hand over the cookies and nobody gets hurt."

He spun, capturing my wrist in his free hand with a hard slap, holding my fingers safely away from his body.

I smiled into his pissed-off blue eyes. "It's alright. They're not loaded."

"Diamond. I knew it." His voice was a whisper, soft and cool as the evening. He released my wrist, changing his grip to the back of my neck. Then his mouth, hard and scorching, was on mine.

One kiss. One moment. It was all we needed.

He set the bag on the picnic table. "Here's your damn cookies." He pulled out the Walkers and tossed them to me.

Next came the bottle of his favorite scotch. He opened it without ceremony and drank. "Fuck, you drive me crazy. What's with the games?"

"That's my line."

"What are you talking about?"

"Hanna Lang and her kidnapped fiancé Damon Marten. You remember him, the guy you and Popov are sitting on in your cottage."

His eyes widened for an instant. It was enough to confirm my suspicions.

"You ass. You set me up to babysit her because you didn't think I'd find you. You planned to have me chasing ghosts, keeping Hanna too busy to make noise while you sat up here and pulled strings. I knew it. I'm going to kick your ass using good ol' number forty-seven." I set my cookies down and grabbed the scotch. He didn't let go. We devolved into two-year-olds. I pulled. "Give me that."

He pulled harder. "No."

A bullet hit the sidewalk a foot from me. "Seriously? I'm gonna kick Popov's ass, too. Where the fuck is he?"

Another bullet ricocheted off the pavement and into a cluster of trees.

"Down. Down." The Russian assassin burst from those same trees, urging us across the road behind the cover of the stone wall separating us from the canal.

"Damn it, Diamond. What did you do now?" Irish spat the accusation while he armed himself.

I did the same. "Me? This is your fucked-up game, buddy, I'm just your pawn."

"Diamond?" Popov looked at me for the first time. He took in the wig, then stared into my eyes. Happiness was a broken-toothed smile. "Yes. I was so bored I considered putting a bullet in my own head. Now, life will be interesting. Who were they shooting at?"

"Her," Irish said.

"Him," I said simultaneously. "Where is it coming from?"

"Stick your lovely neck out and I'll watch for the next shot," Irish offered sweetly.

I stuck my tongue out at him.

"Seriously," Popov said, nudging me higher. "Do it. They are a horrible shot. You should be safe."

"Why's it always me?"

Irish grinned. "You're a people person. People are always trying to kill your person." Just as quick, his smile faded. "Nothing better happen to you. I'll be using number sixty-seven."

I rolled my eyes. "You don't even know what sixty-seven is. Spread out, I'll draw their attention. You two make mincemeat out of them."

It had been no more than sixty seconds since the last shot. I edged toward an opening in the wall as the men worked their way toward the main street. A sign welcoming boaters to Fort Augustus provided a screen for them.

"Hello thar, lass. Needing help, are you?" My former picnic table mate bellowed from the restaurant doorway.

"Get back inside. Now."

"Why would I be doing that?"

I waved my hands at him, shooing away the collateral damage. I heard the shot this time. The bullet splintered the top rail of a fence.

"Call the coppers, lads! Call the coppers!" The door slapped against its stops, and I was alone.

Another shot fired. A different gun. I twisted toward Irish and Popov. It had been Irish who fired. He signaled me to him. Then we were on the move. "Shooter was on the chapel across the canal. They vacated at my shot."

"Did you get him?"

"Not likely. Bad angle. He can't be a pro. We were dead in his sights. Still winds. Good light. If he were a pro, we'd be ghosts."

We came to the end of the walk. To get to the chapel, we had to cross two bridges. The first one over the river had stone parapets elbow-high. Good cover. The second one over the canal had wire mesh for side walls. Very exposed. One way or another, we had to move. Sirens were coming our way.

Guns discreetly at our sides, we moved quickly, weaving in and out of pedestrians, not leaving clear shots.

The small stone building with steep peaks wasn't a chapel, at least not anymore. By day, it sold crafts. By night, it apparently cloistered far-sighted killers. A ladder still leaned against the back of the building. Popov monkeyed up, clearing the roof, while Irish provided cover. Inspecting the ground fell to me. The challenge of the job was that the not-a-chapel was in the middle of the beaten path. The one in front was the foot access to The Boathouse and The Highland Club as well as a tiny coffee shop and a Loch Ness boat tour business. Behind the building was a stoned area working as ad-hoc parking. The ground was dry but not hard. At the base of the ladder were two distinct imprints, as if someone landed hard, then pivoted.

"Got a print," I told Irish. "Stay where you are." Popov's military tread already overlapped the edge of the much smaller shoe. Two strides leaving the ladder were distinct in the gray, sandy dirt. Two strides was all it took to be in vegetated ground cover. Retracing the steps, I found three prints coming in from the beaten path to where the ladder must have originally laid.

I lined my foot up against the most distinct print. It was the same size, making our shooter around five foot ten. I photographed the prints. Old habits.

Two minutes later, Popov rode the ladder down. "Asshole definitely used the roof. Fresh breaks on a few tiles, which caught some black fibers. Found some crumbs, too. Asshole had a snack. Disgraceful. Gives the profession a bad name." He pulled a small plastic bag from his pocket, showing two stringy puffs of black. Opening the closure, I rubbed them between my fingers. Soft. Ordinary. They could have come off three different shirts I owned or any of the five black hoodies Dix lived in.

The crumbs were a buttery tan mixed in with grit in shades

of gray. I rubbed these between my fingers, too. The crumbs, well, crumbled, the grit did not. They were too small to have a discernible scent. I put it to my tongue, remembering too late how Euro Rat had done the same thing. God, I hope my insides weren't about to melt. Saliva pooled in my mouth, a reaction to a welcome taste. "Asshole was eating Walkers."

Irish snickered. "Proves he was shooting at you."

"Proves he had taste if not a good eye."

Popov pointed his chin to the string of small businesses across the street. "We can check there for witnesses. All the ones around here are closed."

The sirens arrived across the canal. Two cars pulled in front of The Moorings, guided in by my former picnic table mate. His hands flew like an Italian as he laid out the scene.

In silent agreement, we obscured evidence of our own presence and faded into the foliage. We fell into formation, moving quietly through a short stretch of dense trees and shrubs. Over a forgotten wire fence and we were back on Highland Club grounds.

"You and your shortcuts," Irish scoffed in a London accent.

"Why do we ever follow you?" Popov said in a matching cockney.

I snorted and showed off my own linguistic talent. "Men always follow women. It's the destiny of the cock."

And so, we three tourists wandered around the property to Irish's cottage. "Surprised to find you here, Popov. Fort Augustus is a little tame for your tastes."

"Am babysitting professor," he said, sounding as if being punished.

"Below your paygrade. What did you do?"

"When superior gives you bottle of his family vodka and asks for honest opinion, is a trap."

An official car turned into the parking lot just as we closed the cottage door behind us.

"What the fuck!" Irish swore as he stormed through the living area to the kitchen. He lost the packaged accent, blustering in his own voice—a mutant mix of Dublin, Belfast, and London. No one in any of the kingdom's countries understood him unless Irish was faking an accent.

I fished out the pins holding the wig in place. Off came the wig and the netting containing my own hair. "Someone followed me. They must have, but how?" Had the TBOs really tracked us? I wanted to deny they could have tailed us without me noticing. Truth was, and you better not repeat this, I didn't give them a thought once we left the castle. Double, I was distracted arguing with Dixon.

"Maybe you are getting soft. Diamond is turning to chalk." Popov stripped off weapons, setting them with care on a table, back to his own unique take on English. "Slow and soft."

Oh, he did not.

I flew at him, taking the big man down to the kitchen floor with a scissor twist. He cursed in Russian. I did the same as we tumbled across the tiled floor. Irish laughed, cheering us, coaching us both. He was fucking Switzerland. I ended on top and rode Popov hard, countering each attempt to throw me.

"Anna? Annalisa, is that you?"

The sound of a new voice. "Don't—FUCK!" I glanced up, a mistake. My back engaged the floor. Hard. "Call me that," I said without breath.

Popov's ugly face loomed. His final blow was in Russian. "Slow and soft, little girl." He left the room, laughing at my expense.

I craned my neck. In the doorway, a confused, familiar face stared down at me. I rolled, coming to hands and knees. "Damon! I knew it!" I climbed to my feet, no help from the "gentlemen" around me.

"Annalisa?" Irish grabbed my wrist, pulling me to his side. "You know each other?" Irritated, he spat out each word.

"Annalisa was my teaching assistant," Damon Marten said. He hadn't changed much in the years since we last met for lunch. His dark complexion seemed to throw off the years, his face still smooth. He still wore his hair cropped close, but salt had started infiltrating the pepper. New were the exhaustion reddening his eyes and the sadness making him frown. "What are you doing here?"

"Looking for you. Hanna hired me." I twisted my wrist, a silent order for my release. Irish complied but didn't give ground.

"Hanna?" Damon said her name in a whisper, as if she was the wish he was afraid to say aloud.

I gave a short nod. "She's here."

"You brought her here?"

"You brought her here!"

Guess which Irish said.

"Where?"

"Where!"

The cottage had an angry Irish echo.

"In a penthouse with Dixon."

"YOU BROUGHT THE KID!"

"You have a kid?" This time, it was American and Russian accents doing double duty.

"Dixon's not *my* kid. Okay, he's mine, but I didn't birth him. Jeeze, he's seventeen. And you three need to back it down. What the fuck is going on? Straight up. No bullshit."

Irish maintained his *I'm-so-pissed-off-I-could-strangle-you* expression. Popov had no expression. Zero. Could have been a statue. Damon looked ashamed. His gaze fell to my shoes.

"I know what happened in Germany, Damon. Jeremy Hardy told me everything."

Damon's chin snapped up. "Jeremy? I...I forgot about him. Did they get him, too?"

"I got him. China Whiting, too."

"Shit." Irish shook his head. "I should have known it was you. You made the news."

"Bad guys found Jeremy fifteen minutes after I did. I had to take extraordinary steps. If Ian's 'friends' hadn't gotten to China when they did, she'd be fish bait, too. What took you so long?"

Irish shrugged. “Paperwork. You know how it is.”

Sadly, I did. It was one of the perks of being dead. No protocols, authorization, or funding requirements.

“I want to see her.” Damon’s declaration had us all looking to the doorway. He stood there with the gun Popov called “Widow Maker.” “I want to see Hanna. Now.”

TWO BLONDES WALKED INTO A BAR, OPENED THE DOOR, THEN TRIED AGAIN

We laughed and laughed. Popov was crying, blinded by the tears running down his chiseled cheeks. Irish planted his butt into the wall, doubling over, arms wrapped around his high-end gourmet shirt. For me, out and in collided for an oh-so-elegant snort. Damon was built for the classroom, down to his bow tie. Put the cold steel in his hand and you had the making of an oxymoron.

"I'm serious," he said in an English so polished, it shined. "You don't think I'll do it?"

"Okay," I said, holding out a placating hand. "I'm sorry. Give me the gun."

"No," Popov countermanded as he wiped his face. "I want to see him try."

Irish straightened quickly. "Fuck you, Pop. This is my house. Marten, give Diamond the gun and you'll get your girl."

Slowly, reluctantly, as if he was giving up his only leverage, he handed it over, butt first. "I would have," Damon said, determined to hold his own.

I accepted it, passing Popov back his toy. "You couldn't have, not holding it that way. It has an automatic safety. Come on, let's go see Hanna. She's been worried." I scorched Irish with a glare, making it per-fect-ly clear I expected an explanation.

"Annalisa." He shook his head, the way you do when you don't trust your eyes. "I can't believe you're here. Of course, you're here. What am I saying? Asa said you were the best he ever trained. I should have called you when this whole thing started."

Asa MacGregor. The man who recruited and trained me. God, his name still made me ache. "I am Diamond." I turned on my heel, stalking to the front door. "Annalisa doesn't live here anymore."

The party moved to the penthouse. I unlocked the door, Irish elbowing to the front and clearing the suite. Hanna stood in the living area barefoot, wet hair hanging heavy.

"Promise kept," I said and stepped aside.

"Damon!" Do I really need to describe how happy Hanna was to see Damon?

I thought not. Leave the sappy shit for romances.

"How are you here?" Arms filled with a damp blonde, Damon's voice strained as if an invisible hand squeezed his throat closed.

"Diamond and Dixon." Hanna pressed her cheek to his chest, her smile broad. She sniffled through the tears of joy rolling unabated. "Diamond got us here. She killed a guy to do it."

All eyes came to little ol' me. All except for Dixon's. He was sprawled across the far couch like a puppy who just fell out where he was.

"It was crazy," Hanna said. "She speared him with a selfie stick and threw him over a wall. He broke his neck on a headstone in a dog cemetery."

Irish's brilliant blues danced in laughter. "Still earning style points, are you?"

"Damn right," I said. "Have to keep up with you. Let's talk about the charade you and Popov are running."

We drifted to the dining table, we five. Irish took the head of the table, Popov to his left. I sat to his right. Damon next to me, Hanna attached to him. The rest was covered with Dixon's tech, which made like rabbits, doubling every time I looked.

Irish and Popov. Where the two went, death rates rose and panties fell. I pinned them both with a look to make grown men piss their pants. "This better be good."

Irish leaned back, unperturbed by my scowl. "Monica Hass was in the employ of the German government. She and Knoll Klemer collaborated on research, speaking often. During their last conversation, he told of a call from a publication interested in their graduate work. They had agreed, long ago it seems, to never speak of it. It began his short trip to the bottom of the Seine. When news reached Hass of Klemer's death, she called her German friends. She had few details and little proof. The Germans called the French." He waved his hand in a slow circle, silently filling in the details. "While a security force evaluated the situation, she jumped off a building. A camera caught it all. Cornered by three men, she looked at the camera and mouthed the words *save them*, then she made her own way out. She had sent what she had to her German contact. Still, it was weeks before we had a direction. The Danube Progressive Bewegung."

Popov rocked back on his chair. "They are small, nationalist group who want a Germany for only those born German. They are attacking places popular with locals, making to appear as Syrians and Turks and others loyal to Russia are killers." The distaste and disdain he had for the group was clear in every word. "British, Russian, French, American. All of us pressured the Germans to act. The signs were neon."

"Neon, yes," Irish said. "But there is little evidence. In our countries, we don't arrest on suspicion of an intent to harm."

Popov snorted derisively. "You wait until coffins being cried over, then go on quest for your justice. In Russia, mothers can rely on the government to keep their children above the ground."

"Oh, not this shite again." Irish planted his palms on the table, rising. Popov mirrored him. Voices and bodies rose in an old argument.

"Really?" I got out of my chair and went mother-may-I on their asses.

Then it was all ouch, Diamond. Feck, Diamond. Jesus, Diamond. Stop, Diamond.

I let them go, returning to my chair. Irish may have been sitting at the head of the table, but I controlled it. "Get to the part of why me, why Hanna. Popov, shut it. Irish, spill."

"Damon was certain Hanna wouldn't be, let's say, accepting of his disappearing."

Hanna sniffed indignantly. Damon instantly answered. "I didn't have a choice. I knew about Knoll and Monica." He cradled Hanna's hand to his heart. "Walking to lunch that day, a woman came up to me and gave me a choice: live or die."

"Sounds like Henderson, a dramatic one she is. Her orders were to get you away. Just you. Mine were to escort you, to hide you, to set you up to work. Popov is security."

"I had no choice," Damon said to Hanna, pleading his case. "Monica had left me an urgent voicemail, I told you about it. I didn't know anything, except she was dead and she thought I could be next. Agent Henderson approached me, proved who she was, ordered me to go with her. She said if I stayed, I'd be a target and, by proximity, you would too. I couldn't let anyone know what I was doing, not even you. I told them I wouldn't lift one damn finger until you were protected. Please believe me, it was the best I could do."

"We're together now. The rest is in the past." Her voice was calm, happy to be reunited, but the glare she cut Irish and Popov was sharp enough to leave body parts on the floor.

What was sticking in my craw was this entire thing was avoidable. "This was a waste of time. Henderson could have taken her."

Irish shrugged. "I had a problem, you provided a solution." Irish focused on me, his lowered head reminiscent of a hound of Baskerville. "You had a problem, I provided a solution."

He surprised me. It showed on my face for a minuscule moment, but long enough he saw it.

"Diamond has a problem?" Popov's brow went Cro-Magnon.

"I left you a message, you bastard." I leapt to my feet, my chair clattering to the floor as I got loud, my overreaction intentional to change the channel on Popov's brainwaves. "One phone call and I'd have taken care of her for you."

Irish rose quietly, a cat readying to pounce. "Bollocks. You'd have pawned her off on your Black."

I dialed it up to eleven. "You'da been better off with him. He'da picked up the breadcrumbs you laid down and said thank you very much. He wouldn't have gone to Calvert. He wouldn't have solved the Lenore puzzle. And he definitely could not have re-created the serum. You, sir, fucked up."

"Annalisa...what did you say?" Damon's voice was soft with disbelief, loud with shock.

What did I say?

The room went electric, the hairs on the back of my neck tingled. The room was dumbstruck...and then exploded in a flurry. Everyone was on their feet. Hands and words and curses flew around the table.

It's not possible, Diamond. Hell to the yes, Diamond. Holy bloody hell, Diamond.

I fought the verbal onslaught with proverbial elbows, Irish my primary target. The arrogant prick. Who was he to get up in *my* business? If he thought—

"What did you do?" Damon gripped my forearm tightly, spinning me until I looked into eyes steeped in sorrow and fear. "Tell me you didn't cross that line."

I felt his disappointment and it was not comfortable. There aren't many people in this world whose opinion of me matters. I can count them on one hand. I wouldn't have put Damon on that list, but the knotting in my stomach, the heat creeping into my face said he was there. They all looked at me. Judging. Pushing me into a corner until my only choice was to fight my way out. "You're worried *I* crossed a line? Let's talk about you, Damon. Everything you taught me about respect and boundaries and morals, it was all bullshit. You hammered me over and over, year after year. Discipline. Do no harm. Create, not destroy." I got in his face, finger to his chest. "You were lucky all you wiped out was a flock of birds."

Damon stepped forward, not back, his voice cold. "Everything I taught you was because of what we did. What *I* did. I had to learn the hard way the consequences of thinking you knew better than everyone else. I wanted to give you, all my students, the benefit of my experience. You have no idea the scars I carry. It was a hard, painful lesson to learn. Yes, I hammered you because you, of all my students, were the most dangerous. You were smarter, more confident, and refused to quit. I did what I could to protect you from yourself."

The blow stung as much as if flesh had connected with flesh. I pulled off the gloves and went for the throat. The best defense was a fucking killer offense. "Because you were so wise? Keeping the formula. Leaving the clues. Giving me that fucking Poe collection. You practically dared me to walk in your footsteps. You're just pissed I perfected what you couldn't."

My face burned then. Literally. The crack registered an instant later, the sharp slap of Damon's hand to my face. Righteous fury burned in those brown eyes. Well, welcome to the neighborhood, pal. He wanted to play, then I would—

"Stay still." It was Irish's voice in my ear, his hand wrapped over my fist. "Popov, take them to the cottage." He pulled me away from the table; I let him. It was the only thing I could do to stop the urge of retaliation driving my nails into flesh.

Damon went to Popov, Hanna in tow. He hesitated in the doorway, looking over his shoulder at me. "I expected more."

The part of me that acts before I think took a step forward. "I expected—"

"Get them out of here, Pop." Irish snapped the order, his free hand over my mouth. When the door closed, he let me go. "You can thank me later." He crossed to the second couch, dropping into the soft cushion. "You never fail to impress me with the amount of trouble your mouth can cause."

"Oh, please. My mouth is world-renowned for its talent and creativity." He laughed and the last of the tension broke. Admittedly, that little scene was not the grateful reunion I expected. And now Damon and I were at odds. Damn it. How was I going to bridge this gap?

Pacing in a broad circle, I shook my hands to dispel the adrenaline build-up. More or less back to normal, I crouched down next to Dixon, who'd slept through it all. His smooth face was completely relaxed. Long, feathery lashes laid in a dark crescent. He snored softly.

"Guess he finally crashed." I brushed away the few strands of hair falling across his lips. He didn't stir. "I was beginning to think it wouldn't happen. He just kept going."

"You can Lazarus from your own grave but not rally your Dixon? I have to rethink my opinion of your superpowers." He patted the seat next to him. "Did you really make the serum? Marten has been working night and day with little to show except supply lists. Each day comes with a new list."

Interesting. "I had help." I sat next to him, close without touching, both of us watching Dixon. Something about his sleep of the dead didn't sit well. "He seem normal to you?"

"The boy has taken to hanging with the likes of you, there's nothing normal about him. Tell me about this man you killed."

We briefed each other on our separate missions. Irish asked detailed questions about our time in Edinburgh with no insights into how someone tracked me to Fort Augustus or who that someone was. There also were no new revelations on Irish's part. Together, Ian, Dixon, and I had gotten the generalities right. He swore on the life of his wee Gran that he didn't know Damon and I had a past.

I was still fifty-fifty on believing him.

"What comes next?" he asked.

"Good question. My job is done. Technically." Hanna and Damon were reunited, true. Yet with the TBOs and the Raven serum and this Danube Progressive Bewegung, the job didn't feel done. "But."

"Exactly." He rose, a pensive look on his face. "We'll talk. I'm going to the cottage and making dinner. Bring your bottomless pit by in an hour."

"All right." When the door closed, I started the process of waking a teen. "Dixon, time to wake up. Come on, you aren't going to be able to sleep if you sleep too long." God, I sounded parental. When calling him, shaking him, and ordering him didn't work, I put my back into it, bouncing him up and down. "Wake up, damn it."

He smiled. "Higher. I wanna go higher."

"Higher?" He was dreaming. Still, "Come on Dix. You're freaking me out." I snagged a pillow off the other couch and hit him across the back. Not mean. Well, not too mean. "Wake up. Wake up. Wake up."

And one eye slowly opened, raising to half-mast.

"Hello in there. Earth to Dixon."

His smile was broad, dopey, like he was half stoned. "Diamond. What time is it?" His words were garbled amid a crocodile yawn.

"Dinner time. You're going to want to get up before Irish eats all the food." And I had his attention, although it's up for debate if the man or the eats got him to his shaky feet. I grabbed his arm to steady him.

"I'm ready," he announced, sour breath in my face.

I shoved him toward the bathroom. "After you go a round with a toothbrush."

He lifted his arms, stretching. "I need a shower. Maybe after—"

"Before," I said over him. "If it was bad enough you noticed, it is definitely before."

"Check our page. We had like five buyers interested. I had them up to ten million. Is that sick or what?"

And my head glitched like it does with Dix sometimes. "We have a web page? Five buyers? Ten million?"

"On the dark web, I set us up, we're independent. Posted we had something juicy to sell. Just, look." He went to the dining room table and roused one of the laptops. Some wicked fast clicks on his keyboard and I was looking at a rock glowing red, orange, and yellow. Below was the tag line "Weapon of the Milenium." Yep, even spelled it wrong, but he had offers climbing up to ten million.

"What is that a picture of?"

"A rock I picked up from Loch Ness. I filtered it." He tossed me the actual rock. It settled nicely in the palm of my hand—pretty, with striations of white, grey, and dark grey.

"These can't be legit." I nudged him out of the way to see for myself if people out there were nutters enough to bid ten mil on a radioactive rock and a typo. "Go shower, I want to look at this."

"'K." He started off, then turned. "I get a part of it, right? The ten mil."

I raised my eyes to a face broad with adventure and pride. "Fifteen percent of the final price. Standard finder's fee."

"Fifteen? That's...holy shit, that's a lot of money." Then he was running, leaping to slap the frame over the door.

Let's see what he had. Okay, the typo hadn't put any of our buyers off because four of the five used the phonetic English dictionary. Dixon had begun five separate chat lines, doing a very nice job of playing the buyers off each other. The description of the effects of Raven were his interpretation of my description. Truth serum. Bleeding eyes. Melting guts.

By the time Dix reappeared, wet hair hanging in his eyes, I had baited all five. My gut said two were cops, and three were legitimately illegitimate, one of which was so far out of his league, he was in the wrong stadium. One was especially eager and had a representative in my vicinity. I've already given you my opinion on coincidences, which is to say I have a date tonight.

Until then, might as well eat.

Popov opened the cottage door as we approached, his hard gaze strip-searching my chief technology officer. "Popov, this is my Dixon." I stepped into the living room where Damon and Hanna sat together on the couch. Irish was beyond, in the kitchen, drying his hands.

"I'm...I'm with her." Dixon ducked past Popov. He was only a few inches shorter but tipped the scales about fifty pounds less.

"Awake, is he?" Irish stepped into the living room, a teasing smirk on his face.

Now, worth description was how happy Dixon was to see Irish. Before all of this, Irish had come to my building a few times. I worried about their meeting. Dixon, my deviant, guardian angel, had pointed the cops at Irish's house by calling in a fake hostage 9-1-1. Irish, pissed that someone had the balls to swat him, demanded those balls on a platter. The baby bull charged the badass bull head-on and survived. More than. Irish respected Dixon. Dixon idolized Irish.

Which couldn't be a good thing. But I digress.

Dixon took three Superman steps, launched off the coffee table, bounced off a couch cushion, leapt the couch back, narrowly missing the snuggling Damon and Hanna, and skidded to a stop at Irish's toes. Dixon didn't hug him, but his hands flapped at his sides like a seal begging for fish. A consequence of his childhood, Dixon wasn't comfortable touching and was averse to being touched.

"Nimble punk." Irish blew past Dixon's issues, bringing him in for a one-armed guy hug. He delivered a hearty slap to the back and then they stood, side by side, Dix's neck in the crook of Irish's arm. The latter looked at me, his head cocked toward Dix. "Was you who found me?"

"Yeah, well, I mean, I found you and tracked you to the airport. Diamond did everything from there. She was kinda pissed at you."

"I bet she was." Irish ran his tongue between his teeth. "Next time, let's have you call me, not Mother."

"Mother?" I repeated, mentally putting a knife to his carotid.

"You think there's going to be a next time?" Dixon asked

hopefully. A timer went off interrupting, but the set of Irish's pursed lips was answer enough.

Damon rose from the couch, extending a hand to Hanna. "Dinner is ready."

After the dinner plates were cleared, Irish and Popov went into Fort William, taking Dixon along. Apparently, something needed picking up that warranted six hands. Man hands. This left me the badass on duty. I was lethal three times over and connected into Irish's custom surveillance system. The cottage was quiet. I passed the time with Detective Chief Inspector Barnaby, who was knee-deep in another murder in the deadliest place in the United Kingdom: Midsomer.

"I'm sorry, Anna—Diamond." Damon inserted his body between me and the televised corpse. "You're going to have to be patient with me. Like I was saying, I'm sorry I snapped. The stress of the situation is getting to me. Fear something would happen to Hanna." He looked to the kitchen where she was putting away dishes. "Thank you for bringing her."

Apparently, we were going to talk about this now. I turned down the sound, using the moment to frame my mind. I didn't want to be at odds with Damon. I wanted his respect back. "You don't have to thank me. I'm sorry it took as long as it did for us to find you. It's easy to see what you mean to each other."

"I love her." He sank onto the couch. "It killed me when they said I couldn't bring her."

"Tell me how this started? Why were the feds protecting you but not Jeremy Hardy and China Whiting?"

"My research is sponsored by the U.S. Army. I took Monica's warning seriously and called the colonel overseeing my project. I expected to have to leave, to work from one of the bases. I packed bags for the two of us. I wanted to be ready. That agent, Henderson, surprised me. Then she said Hanna couldn't come. She didn't care that Hanna would be a sitting duck for anyone who came looking for me. She didn't care. When I was alone with Irish, I begged for his help."

His story filled in a few gaps. It explained the duffle bags I found in their condo and some of the cloak and dagger. Irish was lucky. Without explanations, I was going to go number thirty-nine on him the next time we were alone.

"I'm glad Irish sent Hanna to me. You stuck your neck out for me, all those years ago. This gave me the chance to return the favor."

"You give me too much credit." Damon rubbed his hands over his face. "I can't believe you re-created it."

Pride made me smile. "I did. I'll admit I had help. I couldn't have done anything without your formula, and Jeremy Hardy remembered enough to keep us moving."

He laughed, but it was with derision, distaste. "Jeremy, of all people, should have known better. He was the only one smart enough to walk away the first time." He opened the flood gates, talking about the worry someone would re-create the serum, the abject fear of it being used, and the anger that gripped him when he understood I had done both. "You shouldn't have done it." He lashed out, tearing apart the truce we had built.

Voices rising, Hanna came into the room.

"You shouldn't have left the process hiding in plain sight."

"It was not in plain sight." He stubbornly refused to accept his share of the responsibility but had no trouble issuing orders. "Tomorrow, we're working on a neutralizer."

"Fine with me. Seeing what it could do, an antidote is a must."

"We'll have to analyze the components to determine the counter." He paced across the thick area rug as murder played out on the small screen behind him. "It may take you some time to find the digital resources."

Because, naturally, I would be the assistant. It was going to have to get through his thick head, one way or another, I was no one's sidekick. "You're the Ph.D.;, research is your alley, not mine."

I had the epiphany that, though he knew I worked for the CIA, he never stopped seeing me as younger, growing, maturing. Maybe I had still thought of him as knowing, leading, infallible. Time had changed us both.

He frowned, rejecting my rebuttal. “We’ll see. Describe what happened to those men in my office. Every detail.” My description was clinical, focused on the reactions as clues to possible antidotes. Still, he became agitated, shaking his head, denying the facts. “It wasn’t supposed to be like this. What we made was supposed to save lives.”

Hanna went to him, took his face in her hands. “This isn’t your fault. How many people see pain and suffering and try to stop it? Very few. Prevent it? Even fewer. You do not apologize to anyone. Do not let their politics, their problems, drown you. You are too good for them. You don’t need them.”

He rested his forehead against hers. “You are the only one I need.”

The intensity of their emotion swamped me. I turned away from the pair, going to the front window. Looking out, I focused all my attention on the parking area.

Audi. Light. SL68LKS. Silver 68 Lakes.

BMW. Dark. SX19FWR. Sex 19 Forward.

Ford. Dirty. YB69JDY. Why be 69? Enjoy the Day.

“Disagree,” I finally said, turning to face the couple. “You need us. All of us. You’re in up to your eyeballs, Damon. You two are reunited, sure, great, but four people are dead. More injured. You, Jeremy Hardy, and China Whiting are still on the most wanted list of a group willing to go to extremes for the information in your heads. You can’t walk back into Calvert and pick up where you left off.” True statement, regardless of the fact I burned it down.

“I can’t go back to teaching?” His brows dipped between sad eyes. “I hadn’t thought that far.”

“Don’t worry so much, Damon. We have options.” Hanna’s gaze came to me, her chin rose in defense of her man. “The formula is in your head, too."

"True, but they don't know that. You're right that there are options. Maybe one of the agencies has a plan for you. Maybe we find an alternative. Look, relax for the night. You're safe here. Tomorrow, we'll put our heads together. Okay?" They reluctantly agreed. Just as my pep talk ended, a car pulled through the gated entrance. The plate showed clearly on my cell. Irish was back. "The guys are back. I'm going to get a little work done."

Irish's car kicked up rocks as it slid into the parking lot. A rear door opened, and Popov's ugly head appeared. They must have tied one on because he did not look well.

"They're all yours. I'm off duty for the night." I left the cottage and was in the penthouse only long enough to dress for the night. I wanted to be miles away when anyone came looking for me. The base layer would help regulate my body temperature and keep the girls in check if I ended up running around. The middle layer was a cadre of holsters and sheaths. Nothing large, nothing traceable. The frosting was a white blouse and black dress pants, both with a flowing drape and invisible slits providing access to my weapons. I selected the red wig again, covering my short black hair. The black raincoat was more about function but looked kick-ass. I did my makeup, finally packing the small bag that converted from shoulder bag to backpack.

I drove the curves up the A82 to Inverness to a pub set along the river, situated among shadows and alleys. I had used the pub for meetups before, but it had been years. I wanted to be early, to have time to get reacquainted with the potentially game-changing shadows.

Inverness isn't so different from any other city. Some things change but more stay the same. The change, in this case, was a busy pedestrian way with more witnesses than I liked on this summer night. The same was Kevin, bartender and owner of The Crane and Thistle, his whiskers grayer, his lines deeper than half a decade ago. While the proprietor may have resembled the pub's namesake in his youth, his girth now was more reminiscent of penguin than crane.

"Hello, Kevin," I said, slipping on a stool, a friendly smile for the familiar face.

"That'd be me. Do I know you, lass?" He wiped the bar in front of me, studying my face.

"You did, about five years ago." I slid into a coquettish grin. "Have I really changed so much?"

"Scarlet?" His full belly laugh filled the small bar. "Well, I'll be damned. What kind of trouble have you been up to these past years?"

"Only the best kind."

"Are you still associating with the bastard from Belfast?" he asked, referring to one of Irish's aliases. Like many in the UK, Kevin had a good-natured dislike of the other countries. It reminded me of the way we poke fun at neighbors over the state line. I'm proud to claim Maryland as my home state, but that didn't stop me from feeling bad for my Virginia neighbors when they no longer had ice. The woman who had the recipe died.

See? All in good fun.

"I finally took your advice, dropped him in the Thames." And now I had number one hundred one for the list.

And he laughed again. "That'll teach him, dirty water'll take the skin right off." He drew a pint I didn't order and set it in front of me. Kevin introduced me to my neighbors and returned in between customers, keeping the pint in front of me full.

Thus completing my cover. I laughed and told stories, a small part of a big crowd, all the while using the mirror in front of me to watch the room. Twenty minutes after me, who walked in the room? TBO2 and TBO3. Because they were tall, blond, and obvious, everyone knew they didn't belong in the local pub.

"What do we have here?" Kevin drew a pint, stopping it on instinct as his gaze went to the outsiders.

I glanced over my shoulder. "Looks like paying customers to me."

"Aye." He set the pint in front of my neighbor. "Maybe."

They ordered pints, minding their own business. Kevin checked in with his staff, who had fewer complaints about the TBOs than the quartet of tourists who weren't holding their liquor half as well as they thought they were.

"Don't like the looks of 'em." Kevin had good instincts.

"Find out when they arrived, where they're staying." When his gaze flashed to me, connecting my appearance to theirs, I shrugged. "Just in case there's trouble."

At his direction, the older woman on his wait staff chatted them up as she delivered fresh pints. Margaret was the perfect mole, looking like a cross between a nanny and your favorite aunt. They asked her questions, ones she took her time answering before sweeping away the dirties.

They had just arrived from Edinburgh and were looking for a place to stay. Hunger and thirst had gotten the better of them. Margaret steered them to a small hotel around the block, run by Kevin's wife's family. As time ticked away, they became more focused on the room, leaving half-finished glasses on the table.

Eleven o'clock, I texted the number I had using a burner phone. *You showed. Congratulations, you have my attention.* Send.

The heads that had been not-so-subtly searching the room snapped down to the screen on the table. Then they were combing the room again while I stood and leaned over the bar, perusing Kevin's inventory.

When I sat, a message waited. *Where are you? Come join us.*

Thanks, but no. You could be coppers.

Their reflections laughed. TBO2 texted. *We are not police.*

Said every cop ever. Until I know you and your money are real, this is close enough.

Our money is real. We are the Danube Progressive Bewegung. DPB has wealthy patrons and ten times your price in our banks.

It felt like cheating, having a battle of wits against unarmed men. Everyone knows you don't count your money while you're sitting at the table. Showing off your chips is only daring me to take them. I did appreciate them confirming their affiliation, saved me a step.

TBO3 stripped the device from his partner. *How do we know the serum is real?*

Ask Mirko.

The pair looked at each other, shaking heads. *Who is Mirko?*

The Euro Rat Karl sent after Damon Marten.

TBO2 frowned as he pronounced *Euro Rat*. He knew Mirko and didn't approve of the nickname. What would he think if he knew his?

How is Karl?

You know Karl?

I know him. He doesn't know me. Not yet, but for this size deal, he will. Nonnegotiable.

For ten mil, we require demonstration.

Fair enough, but you're in a bidding war. Ten mil was the price two hours ago. But I like that you're here. Two now, ten on delivery, and Raven is yours.

The blond heads were secreted in conversation. Their body language said this negotiation just got above their paygrade. TBO2 cursed, the German long and cruel. TBO3 elbowed him, realizing attention turned their way. Both took another slow tour of the full pub. Their gazes brushed over me like searchlights across a telephone pole. *Who are you?*

*I was the student assisting Klemer, Hass, and the rest. The one they didn't notice. The one whose name did not appear on the papers. You can call me...*Drum roll, please. *Peter.*

The texting bubble undulated. Thinking. Thinking. *Peter?*

Peter Piper. Tell Karl the offer is good until noon tomorrow, local time. Once the deposit is made, you'll have your demonstration within twenty-four hours. Then Karl and I can meet and finish our business. I'll be in touch. Then I turned the phone off.

They stayed at their table, fingers busy on the device.

I laid money on the bar, setting my glass on top. "Good to see you, Kevin."

"Come back soon. Me wife will be sorry to have missed ya."

Across the street, I stepped into thick shadows a red-headed woman in a black coat. A minute later, I walked out an ebony-haired woman in navy blue. I crossed the street, turning toward the hotel. The TBOs came out of The Crane and Thistle a few steps behind me. They made no attempt to keep their voices down, assuming no one of consequence would hear.

For the record, I am always of consequence, but I speak English, Russian, Spanish, and French. Not German.

I picked up a few words. Very few words. Peter Piper. Mirko. American. Karl. Leo. The last two were used several times.

They overtook me at the corner, polite as they stepped around me. "Excuse, miss." It was said in English.

They stopped at a Vauxhall Astra. Blue. LE20PTB. Leader20 Peterbilt. I kept walking, no excuse to do otherwise. There was a small restaurant across from the hotel. I sat in the window, sipped coffee, and picked at something passing itself off as dessert. I texted Dixon. After a brief delay in response, he sent the bank transfer information. A refill later, the TBOs had not left the hotel, but we had a deal. The terms were accepted, the transfer would be made when the host bank opened.

All in a good night's work.

The hour drive back to Fort Augustus gave me alone time to figure out my "demonstration." This wasn't a little question. It was worth twelve million. It would keep Dixon in tacos for the rest of his natural life.

Between me and you, I did bring the Raven with me. Not the serum—Jeremy did destroy that in the fire. I brought a quantity of the crystal, one step away from Raven. It was my advantage; I wasn't leaving it locked in Ian's vault. I could use it, give the TBOs their demonstration, and maybe do a little cleanup at the same time, but I wasn't looking to instigate an international woman hunt. My goal remained simple, if not easy: unravel Damon from the knot of international intrigue to give him and Hanna the chance at a life.

I didn't *actually* have to execute a mass attack, I just needed whatever I did to look like one.

Hmm, that may be harder.

As I made the final sweeping turn into Fort Augustus, I had the makings of a plan. Take one festival, mix in a cadre of mobile phones and a dozen bodies. Add blood and gore to taste.

The result? A wicked demonstration.

It would take a team to pull off. My crew was heavy on testosterone, which was fine when a problem required a sledgehammer. I needed tact, grace, and believability. A glance at the dashboard and some quick math said it was still evening in the States. Trixie answered on the first ring.

BOATERS, NOT JUST FOR BREAKFAST ANYMORE

I parked outside the cottage where lights blazed in what had finally become night. Through the picture window, the small living room was comfortable and inviting. One of the couches faced the window. Behind it was the dining table large enough for eight. Three sat at it. Dixon, Irish, and Popov laughed together, in plain view of anyone who cared to look.

So much for security experts.

Still, I smiled as I walked in, wanting some of their happy for myself.

"Irish is…good!" Dixon made the call as though Irish had just stolen second. "You're up, Pop." Dixon sat between the two, at the head of the table, a bottle in his hand. Empties littered the table, fallen soldiers on an abused battlefield. "Oh, hey Diamond. We're seeing who's the best drinker, an Irishman or a Russian." Dix turned back to the contestants. "Irish is in the lead."

"For the moment," Popov said in an English thick with accent and alcohol. "Pour."

"I did," he said, pushing the shot closer to Popov.

"Oh. Good boy." He lifted the glass in salute to his opponent, saw me, and shifted everything in my direction. "To the lady," he said—I think it's what he said—then he downed it. "Ha! Even."

Dixon collected the two glasses, refilled them. "First, they did pull-ups." He pointed to the newly bent steel bar that had previously been part of the cottage's defense system and held the curtain over the living room window. "Popov won with fifty-two."

"Cheated, he did! The fucking bar broke on me, didn't it." Irish turned, noticing me for the first time. "Diamond, me love. Kiss." He puckered up, eyes closed, thoroughly toasted.

"Curtain rods, even industrial-grade, were not made for your fat asses." I gave him his kiss, laughing at the drunken grin I got in return. I picked up one of the empties. "At least you're using good tequila."

"'Tis only fair." Irish waved his hand toward the other side of the table. "He suckled vodka off his ma's tit."

Popov nodded, narrowly avoiding planting his forehead into the table. "'N his baby bottle was half whiskey. Tequila is...is...what is word?"

"Neutral?" Dix said.

"Exactly! Neutral spirit. Pour, boy."

Dixon did, sloshing the clear liquid over the sides.

"How much have you drank?" I asked him.

"Just one." He pushed the drinks in front of the contestants. "It's been more fun watching them. They had contests. Popov won pull-ups, push-ups, and dips. He broke one of his chairs. Irish won target shooting—regular and between the legs—and knife throwing." He pointed to the poor excuse for a circle drawn on the kitchen cabinet and the six knives nowhere close to the middle.

"Don't forget kissing," Irish said sloppily. "Irishmen are best for kissing."

"Nyet, no, nope." Popov planted palms to the table and forced his body to stand. "Russian kiss melts snow. I show you." He lumbered around the table, a top-heavy zombie with dazed eyes trying to focus on me. "Stop moving."

Dixon's eyes darted between me and Popov, his mouth open in a wide grin. Irish rose with no more grace than Popov, shook his head, then grabbed onto the table to stay upright. "Fuck."

Didn't that say it all.

Popov rounded the last corner. He really was an ugly man, but something in the set of his too-oft broken nose and heavy brow was endearing. I let him come, curious how this would play out. His groping hands found my shoulders, clumsily moving up until a large hand cupped either side of my face.

"No hands!" Irish slapped the table. "Be keeping those in your pockets."

Popov dropped his left hand into the pocket of his hoodie. His right flipped Irish off before being tucked away. He bent his head, his shoulders curling forward to accommodate the height difference. He pursed his lips, shut his eyes, and closed the distance between us. His lips met my cheek, and he kept coming. My hands to his shoulders, I backstepped, trying to get control of the two hundred fifty pounds coming down on me. "Popov!" My butt hit the back of the couch. Over we flipped over in a tangle of arms and legs and curses.

Couch cushion. Coffee table. *Crunch.* Floor.

"You've broke me fuckin' table!" Irish flapped around like a bay gull, making a lot of noise but doing no good.

"The table is destroyed." Dixon squatted down, joyfully measuring the destruction.

Someone was looking out for me. I landed on top of Popov instead of being the jelly squishing out between the bread. The legs of the table had blown out, dropping the tabletop onto the thin shelf, and then both into the hardwood floor.

"Yuri?" I propped myself up, patted his broad chest. "You good?"

A soft rumble verified he was alive. Passed out, but alive.

Irish took my arm, pulling me to my feet. "Did he kiss you?" My leg was trapped under Popov. Getting free was a matter of intimate extraction. Irish saw the problem and lifted Popov's leg, swinging it high and wide. "Don't lie to me and say he was better."

I climbed to my feet, looking down at the wreckage. Popov snored atop a pile of kindling. Good thing he had a hard head. Clumsy fingers captured my chin, turning until I looked into merry blue eyes. "The kiss?"

"He didn't—"

"The champion," Irish shouted, grazing me as he thrust fists to the air. "We are the champions, my friends." He butchered the Queen classic. Dixon covered his ears. A nearby cat howled, mistaking him for a mate. Irish kissed me between verses. Dixon saw what was coming and put the dining table between him and the drunk Irishman. Unperturbed, Irish picked up the last two shots, spilled half on the table, the other half down his throat. "I am the champion"—air drums—"of the world."

"Proud of yourself?" I asked.

"Certainly." His grin was one-hundred-proof unapologetic.

"Dix, get a pillow and blanket for our Russian friend. He's too heavy to move. Where are Damon and Hanna?"

"At the penthouse. They wanted alone time."

"Okay, you take Popov's room, just don't play with anything. His toys can bite back." With Popov made more comfortable and the living room window covered, Dixon went to bed, taking his laptop with him. That left me with the big winner. I threaded my arm under his shoulder. "To bed with you."

"I love when you talk dirty." He fell into bed, then nearly rolled out of it reaching for his shoes.

I shoved him to his back. "Just lay there. I'll do the work."

He laughed and laughed.

Getting him down to underwear was like playing twister with an octopus. Sweat rolled down my spine as I finally disentangled myself and pulled the cover over him.

"Lie with me, Diamond." He opened his arms, inviting me in. "Share me bed for a sleep."

I should've said no. I should've crossed the chilled grounds, climbed cool stairs to the penthouse, and crawled into my own bed. It would be still and quiet. Cold. Warmth would be in the next room, where Damon and Hanna would be lying together.

"Come. Me arms want to hold you." He was fading fast.

It was one night. The TBOs were tucked away in Inverness. Karl was still on foreign soil. Tonight was the calm before the storm.

I stripped off my pants and shirt. Shed the weapons and their holsters. Down to basics, I climbed into the bed and fitted myself against Irish.

He smelled like I remembered. Mostly. His natural spice mixing with the expensive cologne he preferred. Ignoring the overtones of alcohol, I snuggled closer, absorbing his body heat.

A kiss pressed to my hair. "That's me girl," he said, draping an arm around me. His breathing slowed and then he slept.

Mine wasn't so fast coming. My brain raced through a labyrinth of thoughts. It had been a long day and I was tired. I was in a soft, warm bed. I'd done enough. I ordered my head to turn off, just for one night.

What could happen in one night?

You know that sinking feeling you get when you fuck up? I'm not talking about the knot you get when you just mess up, like the time I asked my new brother-in-law's little sister when the baby was due...and it wasn't.

I mean when you fuck up so bad, that sinking feeling is south of the Mason-Dixon line and you're trying to remember what color underwear you wore and if it'll show.

As I stood, looking at what wasn't here, I'd fucked up so bad that sinking feeling was in my knees, making me wobbly. I dropped onto a living room chair and texted the three men I'd just left. *Secure the cottage. Get to the penthouse.*

Only Dixon responded. Thumbs-up emoji.

Minutes later, all three walked through the door Dixon unlocked. "What's the matter, Diamond? Hey...where's my stuff?"

"Yeah. That's a question."

Irish and Popov spread out. Dixon ran to his room. I sank into a dining room chair. I was, maybe for the first time ever, dumbstruck.

"Hanna and Damon are gone?" Popov said. "Her suitcases are missing?"

"Yeah."

"The master bedroom is empty," Irish added. "All of your things are gone, too?"

"Everything that wasn't on me."

"The serum, the one you made..."

"Yep. That too."

"Fuck." It was in three-part harmony.

Dixon ran back in the room, pulling his hoodie over his head. "They didn't take my clothes, but they took all my tech. That really sucks. Who would do that? All I have left is the little laptop at the cottage for watching videos."

Irish returned to the door, inspected it. "It hasn't been forced. Hanna and Damon let in whoever took them."

"You think they were kidnapped?" Popov shook his head slowly. "There is no sense. Why take clothes? The computers, yes, but—Dix, what has happened to your shirt?"

Dixon, like the rest of us, looked down to his chest. The woven fibers were snagged from the middle of the chest to the belly. "Awwww. This is my favorite hoodie."

"Anything in the pocket?"

He reached in and pulled out a Walkers wrapper and a beige hairband. "That's not mine. I only use black."

This wasn't good. The sinking feeling was in my ankles now, making me want to kick something. Or someone. "Did Hanna borrow your sweatshirt yesterday?"

"No. Why would she?"

"What did you two do after I left to meet Irish?"

"Hanna made me a cup of tea. She said we were in the UK now and I had to do what Romans did. She watched me, like it was important to her. I didn't like it. It had tea things in it, so I drank it fast. I didn't want to hurt her feelings. It made her happy. So, whatever. Then I sat on the couch to work and Hanna was playing on her phone, but that jet lag stuff caught me, like you said. I woke up when you sat on me."

"THAT BITCH!" I roared as I snatched a dirty glass from a table and threw it across the room. I shoved the chair with my foot, sending it skidding across the polished floor and into Irish's hands. "I told you something was weird about him sleeping through our argument."

"Was she the one that shot at us, then? Where did the rifle come from? And where did it go?" A knock came at our door. I shut up, seething with temper as Irish went to the door and opened it. "Can I help you, Constable?" he asked, using his body to block the view in.

"Sorry to disturb," a thoroughly Highland accent said. "A car was stolen from the rear parking lot last night, a tan Audi. I'm asking all the guests if anyone saw or heard anything."

Out went the theory of someone picking Hanna and Damon up. I joined Irish at the door. "I went out around nine. There was an Audi parked next to me. Light-colored. The plate ended with lakes—I mean, LKS. Is that the one?"

"It is. And what time did you return?"

"It was late, maybe one in the morning, but I didn't park in the same lot. I parked on the side by the cabins."

The constable cocked his head. "That's clear on the other side."

"I have a cottage," Irish volunteered. "She came by for a visit."

The constable flashed an understanding smirk as he turned his attention to me. "Did you see anyone lurking about the area?"

"There was a couple walking up the path from the restaurant. I didn't get a good look, just noticed when he laughed. He had a distinct laugh. Snorty."

"Snorty?" When I nodded, he wrote it down. "Were they guests here?"

"I don't know. I don't remember seeing them before, but we

just checked in yesterday."

"We?"

"My brother and I." The constable stepped in, forcing the two of us back. Dix had put the chair back. "I'm Tara Dixon, this is my brother, Andrew."

"Hi. Do you carry one of those sticks like on TV?"

The constable almost looked amused but didn't answer. Leave it to Dixon to solidly define us as tourists. He took our names, of which only Dixon's matched the one on his birth certificate. Another few minutes of questions we couldn't answer, and Irish closed the door firmly behind him. He waited, listening, then erupted. "That fucking bitch," Irish said with the venom of a copperhead.

"Who's a bitch?" Dixon asked Irish.

"I thought you checked her out," I snapped at Irish, blaming him for being shot at, for all my shit being gone, and for Damon being missing. Again.

"Checked who out?" Dixon asked me. "Whoever kidnapped Damon and Hanna?"

Irish aimed his temper at me. "I thought you were here working. They came back here, under your protection. Where the fuck did you go last night?"

Right. Forgot they didn't know that detail. "I *was* working. Met with a potential buyer for Raven. It was the TBOs, as I suspected. They confirmed they work for Karl Becker and the DPB."

And Popov got his attitude going. "You left Damon with no protection? And you went with no backup while we sit here twiddling fingers?"

"I left Damon under your protection, and I had backup." I lied about the second part. They knew it, I knew it, so it wasn't really a lie. It was more of a de-escalation technique.

"Becker. Huh. That's kinda funny." Dix gave up on us and went to the kitchenette for food. "I guess Becker is a common name in Germany."

I was not in the mood to chase him down a rabbit hole.

"Sure. It's common. Nothing funny about it."

"Hanna's name used to be Becker." He pulled a box of cereal from the cupboard, shook it, put it back, and did the same with the next. "Lang is her married name."

Commencing forward pike dive. "Married?" I looked to Irish. "Did you know she was married?"

"No. Dixon, I'll buy you a case of cereal if you stop and tell us what you know."

"Hanna married this guy, Daniel Lang, when she was my age. Her father was big into his job and Daniel worked for him. Her father really liked him and signed the papers to let them marry before she was eighteen. I think he was like Dickhead." The only name Dixon used to refer to the father who beat him for breathing. "He died. That's why she came to school here."

"She is good. Definitely pro," Popov said.

"Hanna? A pro at what?" Dix wasn't connecting the dots.

"She isn't a woman desperate to find her fiancé," I said. "She's like us, doing a job."

"Hanna? No. Why would she do that?"

"Because these two stole Damon out from under her nose. She couldn't track them, so she created a story and sold it to the first sap who came along." No need to name names. Irish. "The sap decided to play puppet master, sending us on a fool's errand except, uh-oh, we find him. Hanna drugs you, knowing where to set up to take a shot at the competition." I waggled a finger between the white men in the room. "She was shooting at you two. And she did it wearing your sweatshirt, Dix. We reunite her with Damon, they sneak away for some 'private time' stealing a car, taking everything but the shirt on my back, and all your tech."

"But...not Hanna. She likes us." Betrayal cut Dixon to the bone. "We're helping her."

"Just like she wanted. We were played." An alert chimed on my phone. It was a text from my bank. "Well, boys, we're on the clock. The two million has been deposited. I have forty-eight hours to prove the Raven is real."

Popov pounded his fist on the table. "This pity party ends now. Diamond, give me info on TBOs. I will go and find them, put a tracker and mic on them. We will know everything they know."

"Good idea. Karl will be coming in for the deal. Dixon, I need you to do your magic and find Hanna and Damon."

"How? I don't have a computer."

"I'll get you one," Irish said. "Hell, I'll get you five."

"I'll try, but I don't have my back doors here. And there aren't cameras everywhere, like in a city."

"Dixon will come with me," Popov said. "He is good cover."

Dix fist pumped. "Yes! Can I drive again?"

"No!" Popov used his scary voice. "Terrorists are easy. You driving, no."

I shook my head at his poor, poor judgment. "You let him drive? No wonder you looked green getting out of the car. And people say I'm crazy. Look, he's seventeen. He can't go after international terrorists."

"At seventeen, I was shooting wings off squirrels. He will be fine."

"Squirrels don't have wings."

"Because I shot them off."

There was no reasoning with Popov. I tried Dixon. "You're my IT expert. You have skills we need. I can't do what you do. Irish pretends he can, but no, not even close. And Popov can't spell IT."

"In Russian, no. In American, yes." Popov raised one middle finger. "I." Then the other. "T."

Irish stalked between us, taking charge. "Dixon, pack a bag with what you'll need for a day, you're going with Popov." I got the hand of imperial silence. "I want eyes and ears on the two of them. I'll make some calls to get some new equipment and to track the car, but like our boy said, we're in the wilds of the Highlands. My people will dig on Hanna Becker Lang.

Diamond and I will work on a plan to get Damon back and reel in Karl and the DPB."

"Come on, kid," Popov said. "Let's go pillage the cottage."

"Coolio. Irish, I'll send you the background Diamond had me do on Hanna. See ya!" And he was gone.

Popov watched the tornado blow out of the apartment, then turned back to us. "Coolio."

The background on Hanna. I glanced over it. Stupid. Instead of using my own judgment, I relied on Irish's. That sinking feeling dropped into my toes. I hoped Damon wouldn't pay the price for this.

Then Irish and I were alone. "Do they know what they have?"

"No one but you knows I brought any of it. It's in a bottle of bath salts. It's in a crystal form, one step away from deadly. Hanna never saw it in that form. She might not recognize it."

He thought. He sighed. He nodded. "You have a plan?"

"Two-part. I need to get in the lab Damon stocked and craft a placebo. How good is your internet? I'll need to connect with Jeremy Hardy. While I'm doing that, you can make some calls and find me a party. Remember Trixie?"

"The thief? Didn't she start her own company? Cheeky name. What was it?"

"The Cleaning Ladies. I called her in. She's flying into Edinburgh today. She'll need a ride."

"Oh my God! Isn't this beautiful? This, my FB peeps, is the remote side of Loch Ness. No roads, just steep slopes, lots of trees, and the wild side of life." The unseen woman slowly panned the camera. The hillside stretched from the calm water far beyond the scope of the screen. Pines reached high and wide. The gray and white stone lying just beneath the topsoil was visible in washout where water had worn a path, clearing the trees. More rock piled up along the water's edge.

"There's a herd of goats. You see?" The thick, native voice

came from some nebulous place behind.

"Where?" The camera shifted quickly right, the scenery a green blur until it settled on an outcrop. "Found you." The scene zoomed in on three adults and two young ones. "Such thick coats. Look at those horns! They could do some damage." The males featured a pair that arched up and back from the faces, ending in sharp points.

"What's going on over there?" Another woman spoke, her voice smoother, more mature.

Colors blurred by again and we were looking at a small rock beach with three boats tethered to the shore and maybe twenty people shouting and waving to the camera.

"It is most likely a pop-up party." The camera closed in on the group as the guide explained. "*Latha Na Grèine Gun Chrìoch*. Translates to the Day of the Endless Sun. The summer solstice. It is ancient and brand new. People use it as an excuse to be wild. Highlands version of Brazil's Carnival or the New Orleans's Mardi Gras."

"They're waving to us. Can we go?" the younger woman asked. "Mom?"

The debate was short and half-hearted. The captain came into the frame, throwing a rope to a trio waving their arms.

"Steady, lass," the captain said when the videographer stepped to the edge of the boat. "The Loch is deep, the hillside continuing down beneath the water. The earth is still twenty feet below." The shore came closer and closer until the water faded from the scene.

Men and women were in various states of undress, despite the nip in the air. The bottles in hand kept them warm. The camera panned as the daughter called out to the mother. "Point that somewhere else," the mother said, laughing as she stepped behind a young man.

The party was broadcast in high-definition digital glory. The daughter was blonde, dancing in a red bikini. The mother had a deeper golden mane and wore a black bathing suit with a colorful wrap tied around her hips. "Come dance, Captain Tim."

The handsome face smiled shyly from the boat. "I'm fine where I am."

"No," the daughter said, a pout in her voice. "This is your holiday, you should have fun."

He chuckled. "I don't know about that."

Voices rose excitedly. "Did you see?" "I saw something." "No, you didn't." "I did." "There! Did you see? It's Nessie. It's really her."

"Where? Where?" After another whorl of color, the screen panned back and forth across the dark, still water. "Oh my God! I see her. Mom? Are you looking?"

A geyser burst into the air.

Fearfully delighted voices soared over the octaves, rising with the geyser. Then came the sharp pop of fireworks. More screaming. Less delighted than before. The scene streaked across again, the image settling on the last blasts of a short set of firecrackers. Black smoke blended with the breeze, thinning out, wrapping around the partiers like a thin blanket.

"Real funny," the daughter said, then she chuckled. It grew to a laugh as the original partiers began dancing in circles, swooping around the beach with their arms wide like birds. "Mom? Mom! I can't believe you're doing that."

The woman had taken the wrap from her hips and now held it across outstretched hands. "I can fly, Erica! Look, I can fly!"

"Mom! You're not flying!" She scolded teasingly. The camera pitched up. Blue sky. Blue sky. Tree. Another Tree. Tall man. Hands. Blue sky. "Mom? What are you doing?"

Blue sky swept down to gray and white rock, jagged images that changed with each jarring step. The mother came into the bottom corner, her hair spread across the ground. Blood seeped from her nose. "Mom? Oh God. Help. HELP!" The camera fell to the ground, the screen black, the sound very alive. "Tim!"

"What the devil?" the Scotsman gasped. "Holy hell. Get on the boat, lass. Now."

The video was jarring as the daughter ran to the boat. "We can't leave them."

"We have to. This isn't natural." He picked up a radio, calling mayday, reading off their position. Floating some distance from shore, the footage caught the last reveler falling to his knees, then face planting in the sand.

The daughter sobbed. "This can't be happening. This can't be real."

Fade to black.

Behind me, a set of hands clapped. Then two. Then all. I turned away from Dixon's new big-ass screen to the assembled. Trixie the Cleaning Lady, aka the mother, took a bow, then pointed to "Tim," who was none other than our own Sam Irish. Popov had a cameo as Nessie, and Dixon as partier number one. The "daughter" was played by one of Trixie's associates, who was currently returning the theatre students to their university.

I was the director, of course, and had my own role setting the firecrackers and the harmless smoke bomb.

Popov came to the table with two bottles of beer pinched between his thick fingers. He set one in front of Trixie. "You look good in bathing suit."

"Thanks, cutie. You're not so bad yourself." Trixie winked at Popov, casting a line with a single *come hither* look before turning to me. "I can't believe you went for a Loch Ness monster gag, Diamond. When you work for me, you're going to have to class it up a bit."

"I tried to talk her out of it," Irish said. "But she wasn't having it."

"Oh, please. We are on the banks of the fabled Loch Ness. Of course, we were doing a monster bit. And I'm not working for you, Trixie. You're working for me." I handed over an envelope with her fee. "Dixon, you sent this to our buyer, right?"

Our resident IT guru ignored the beer set in front of his underaged ass to root through the kitchen. "Yep. As soon as we got back here, I downloaded, uploaded, and sent." He opened a cupboard, closed it. "Where did all the cereal go?"

"You ate it," Irish said, tipping his chair back. "Same goes for the noodles, the bread, the eggs, and the cheese."

"But I'm hungry."

"You're always hungry. Go clean out your own kitchen."

"He already did," I said. "We have ketchup, mayonnaise, and a few miserable vegetables."

Irish pulled out his wallet. "Go shopping."

"Me?" Dixon squeaked.

"You're old enough to eat like a man, you're old enough to shop like a man." He slapped a hundred euros on the table.

"Sweet!" Dix swooped in, grabbed the bills in his talons, and sailed to the door. "I got this."

Irish shook his head. "God help us if he brings home a week's worth of ramen."

Trixie eased toward the door, ambling, sauntering.

"Diamond." Popov nudged my shoulder. "Keys to the penthouse." He looked at Trixie; she licked her lips.

Two and two equaled four. I handed them over. "Do not use my bed."

His ugly face broke into a crooked grin. "Only soft Americans use a bed."

"I'm not soft," I shouted at his back. And then Irish and I were alone. I heard it then, for the first time.

"It's the loch. Come with me." He led the way to the small porch, cozy with a pair of lounge chairs and a small table. Irish arranged the two side by side, and we sat. The sun warmed our faces as the breeze kept us cool. "We've earned this," he said, linking our fingers, closing his eyes.

I put my feet up on the railing. My boots were heavy on my feet. I gave a thought to changing out of work clothes into something better suited to sitting on a deck, but moving felt like too much work. I copied Irish, relaxing into the padding beneath me. There was nothing but the sound of the wind through the trees, the waves of the lake lapping on the stone shore.

In the moment, my mind was still. I was free. "I could stay here like this." The thought was spoken before I could censor it.

"Aye." He squeezed my fingers. "Scotland is not Ireland, but it has its own magic."

I chuckled, teasing. "You and your magic. No matter what mask you wear, you'll always be Irish at your core." My phone rang. "Probably Dixon. You were nuts sending him shopping." I dug it out of my ass pocket, the number unfamiliar. "Not Dix."

"Your buyer?"

"Probably." I answered, putting it on speaker phone. "You ready to talk details?"

"Details? Does that mean it's true?"

"Damon." Thank fucking god. "We've been looking everywhere for you. Are you alright? Tell me where you are, and we'll come get you."

"I didn't believe it. Hanna told me you were working for the enemy, and I told her no, not you."

"She told you *I'm* working for the enemy. Damon, Hanna is the one playing for the other team. Her brother is Karl Becker, the same guy responsible for Knoll and Monica's deaths." Two days of digging had connected Hanna Becker Lang to her brother Karl Becker. Hanna's husband worked for her father until he died six years ago in a botched attack on a market, brought down by a bullet from security forces. She went to university for four years, worked in a clinic for a year before entering the graduate program at Calvert. The German authorities did not deem her a threat.

Their mistake.

"Hanna is not my enemy." Damon was absolute in his belief. "Yes, Karl is her brother. Yes, he is the one after Raven. Not her. She is making a deal to get us free of him forever. Meanwhile, you are running around, unleashing a chemical weapon on a hapless group of partiers. What were you thinking?"

My eyes met Irish's. We didn't know who was listening on his end. I couldn't tell him it was all a ruse, bait to flush out

Karl and the DPB.

"You have to trust me, Damon. I have one goal here and only one, to get you out of this alive."

There was a moment of silence, an instant of doubt. "But Hanna said—"

"Fuck what Hanna said. You know me, Damon. You've known me since I was nineteen. You know what I'm about."

"I thought I did." There was weariness in his voice this time. "Now? Now you're just like them, using people as your pawns, going for the win, no matter the cost. I'm not going to let you sell Raven to the highest bidder. I will stop you."

"Damon, we're on the same side—" And then he was gone.

"Fuck." I slammed the phone down. "Fuck the fucking fucker."

"Karl must be coming." Irish brought up a mapping app on his phone. "The TBOs remain in Inverness, in a harbor. Maybe Karl is coming by boat. Let's get people looking."

As he searched for contacts, my phone rang again. Dixon. "Vegetables are not a disease, Dix. Do not be afraid."

"Diamond, I need help. The TBOs are here. They're after me."

SIX TIMES THREE MINUS FOUR EQUALS FIFTEEN

Irish sprinted into the cottage. Hand to the railing, I leapt off the porch, taking the shortest path across the property. I ran as I had never run before. The TBOs would not get their hands on Dixon. I'd rip off every finger if I had to.

Meep Meep. The high-pitched whine of a horn made me look twice before stepping on the paved drive. "Get in," Irish shouted, slowing enough for me to jump in. "Where is he?"

"Still at the grocery store." I double-checked my phone. He was still there. At least his phone was.

The gas station slash grocery store slash souvenir shop was less than a half mile from the property. It was longer, having to stay on the roads, but Irish compensated with speed. He took the right on rails, cutting off a tour bus to slide in between cars. A boat was approaching the bridge, but the gates hadn't come down. He pushed the car in front of us to get it moving across. "Get the fuck out of the way." The car surged forward into unoccupied space. We had just cleared the other side when the stop gates dropped, closing off an escape route.

The street was thick with tourists, stretching along sidewalks like children on a field trip. Irish laid on his horn, fair warning as he drifted left, stopping on the curbed island separating the gas station lanes from the driving lanes. One set of gas pumps, two rows of cars stood between us and the small building that was the one-stop shop in Fort Augustus.

Jeers and sneers came our way as we abandoned the car. Two shots came from inside. Pedestrians ducked, then scurried forward or aft. A handful of people scrambled out, streaming around the cars and pumps.

Into the chaos we ran, two fish swimming upstream.

Inside the sliding glass door, Irish went left, clearing the room stacked with spirits. I went right, finding a middle-aged woman trapped behind her pay station. "How many are there? Where?"

"Four men. They're after a boy."

In the mirror behind her, a man stepped into view, assuming a stance made for shooting targets. I dropped, turned, and fired in one motion. Two shots. One to kill. One to dot the i. The woman screamed. I hurried behind the counter, fearing she'd been hit. Lucky her, she was only terrified. With Irish providing cover, we got her over the conveyor belt and out of the store.

"How many?" he asked.

"Three more."

Mirrors meant to deter thieves showed us the battlefield. Aisles were cluttered with exploded cans and tossed boxes. Two victims laid among the detritus, one writhing in pain, the other unnaturally still. Neither was Dixon.

A familiar face leaned into the aisle. TBO2 fired down the alley at us. We dove in opposite directions, the bullets spidering the glass of the sliding door.

Irish signaled to the large arch to his left. I nodded. I couldn't go any farther right. My only option was up one of the aisles.

"This is not what I wanted," I called out in German. My vocabulary was limited to things useful to say at Oktoberfest, but the point was to draw him out, not talk him into surrender. "Let's sit and have a drink."

"*Eine meine seine Deutsch*," he said, or something like that. I didn't understand a word. He kept on jabbering, getting more and more agitated when I didn't respond. He stomped his foot in a tantrum. I took the shot, but my angle was bad. The bullet sliced behind him, embedding itself in a cooler.

Fighting erupted from the next room. Angry shouts of men in the harsh German tones said Irish had found his man. Objects fell to the floor in a heavy rain. A stranger's voice howled.

A barrage of bullets struck in a line above me. I made myself small, less of a target. The soda pop bottles above me did not. They exploded on impact, the pressurized plastic blowing out. Cold, wet, sticky liquid poured down, the plastic tearing at exposed skin. The liter bottles of soft drinks had been hit.

TBO2 faded back, I wasn't sure to where. Two more shots rang out, and this time the voice shouting through pain belonged to Irish.

I hurried toward him on all fours, slushing through the slick soda, my hands and feet slipping with each step. Then I had my feet under me. I rounded a corner and came face to face with a man. A wounded civilian. Shit. "Can you move?"

"My leg." He had dragged his body up the aisle, a bloody trail in his wake. Early twenties, he looked strong with muscles under the high-vis T-shirt. I got under his shoulder and helped him stand. He planted his left boot, but his right leg was dead weight.

"On three." I waited until he nodded. "One. Two. Three." I laid down cover as we hurried across the main aisle, exposed to the adjacent room. I aimed high. Irish was over there somewhere. My man did his part, pushing us faster than I thought he could go, grunting through the pain of each step. It took precious seconds to get him out the door, where his mates took over. "Get to cover and put pressure on the wound."

I went back into the store, this time going left. The souvenir shop was in shambles. Ceramic remembrances of the Highlands laid in shards across the floor where a center shelf had been pushed over.

"Fucking hell." The utterance accompanied the scrape of

metal across the floor. Irish shoved the shelf pinning him, cursing hard and low.

I pushed the damaged goods to the floor, lightening the load. "Where's Dixon?"

"Through the employee door. He has to be there." With Irish pushing and me pulling, we freed him. We fell into old habits, ready to enter the back room. There was shuffling, the sound of something heavy being dragged across the floor.

"Grab him," an accented voice demanded.

Irish pushed the door ajar. My old enemy TBO3 had Dixon pinned in a corner, fists pounding the younger flesh. Dixon learned early how to take a punch. The blows were weakened, glancing off his body. Dixon was fighting back. It wasn't clean and it wasn't pretty, but he was holding his own. Until a new player stalked across the room.

I leapt through the door, striking the new guy in the back. We'll call him TBO4 even though he had dark hair. He fell to the floor, rolling with the momentum. Then I was blindsided. I smacked the concrete floor hard. Bells rang. Stars exploded. But I pushed up as the weight on me lifted, ready to fight back. Irish was already on it, battling TBO2.

TBO4 rose in front of me. Three of him sized me up. I focused on the middle guy, staying balanced while the room spun. Over one of his shoulders, I saw a blurry Dixon land a fast, hard jab. TBO3's head snapped back, but Dixon didn't follow it up.

"Hit him again, Dix." I barked the instruction to get my boy to move. Dixon hadn't been in a fight like this. He had to start playing offensive. "Hit him again and then get out that fucking door."

"You punch like a girl," Dixon said, hitting with words instead of knuckles. And then he screamed. Not shouted. Not yelled. Screamed. He stumbled against the wall behind him, clutching his hip, blood seeping out between his fingers.

"No!" I charged the asshole TBO attacking Dixon. My own non-blond buried his fist in my gut, stealing my air, stopping my charge. I fell back, swallowing the pain, creating space to fight.

TBO3 flipped Dixon around, pinning him to the wall, stilling him with the tip of a blade to his throat. "*Aussteigen*!" He dug his fingers in the base of Dixon's hair tie, then dragged him toward the door at the end of the room.

TBO4 came at me, a sneer on his face, distaste in his eyes. "You'll never see the boy again. You fucked with the wrong people." He led with his right. I turned, taking the blow on the shoulder, his strength knocking me into a line of boxes. Bright and yellow, a box cutter sat three feet away.

TBO4 cracked his knuckles, an unholy grin on his face. "Good night." He pulled his fist back, and my boot planted in his exposed abdomen. While he reeled backwards, I lunged for the utility blade. The warehouse space was a whirl of color and texture as I went momma lion on TBO4. Rage led the way, dark red blood welled, poured from the slashes. TBO4 fought, refusing to go down, refusing to die, taking time I didn't have. I punished him for every second he stole.

Irish pulled me off. "He's done."

"Where is he? Where's Dixon?" The warehouse was quiet. Two hearts beating, two hearts still. Blood pooled around our feet, gravity finishing the job the box cutter started.

Irish's right hand hung limply by his side. "They took him. Come on."

"How bad is it?" I lifted his arm, seeing now the stream of red racing down his arm with the pump of his heart.

"We don't have time."

That was what worried me. I couldn't lose both of them. "Twenty seconds. Get us a plan." Panic was too close to the surface. It was a new feeling. One I did not like. A few Nessie baby onesies layered together made an absorbent pad. Packing tape, shoulder to elbow, put pressure on the damage. "Done."

"I'll go high," he said as we approached the exterior door. We hit it, expecting it to fly open. It didn't. We stood and kicked it together. It wanted to open but couldn't. "They blocked it somehow. The front is our only option."

We raced into the store, skating through the pool of soda, shoving toppled racks out of the way. Once through the shattered front door, we paused to get a beat on direction.

Screams came from our left. A swell of tourists contorted around the violence. Across the road, TBO3, the last TBO standing, muscled Dixon over the short wall that had sheltered me and Irish the day before. TBO3 shouted an order. A man came to attention, another fucking blond, this one in a fishing boat. A motor revved. Then TBO5 jumped to the pier to untie the rope.

Irish and I moved quickly, quietly, using the horde of fearful tourists as cover. When the crowd would take us no closer, we broke rank and ran toward trouble. Guns drawn, we didn't fire. Dixon was too easily caught in the crossfire. TBO5 spotted us, called out to TBO3 as he pulled a gun from under his jacket.

"Get down. Get down," I shouted at the crowd before TBO5 fired. Irish and I dove behind the stone wall. Four shots were fired. No screams or silent gasps answered. His shots buried in the stone wall. A motor roared, the pitch starting high and then fading.

Of one mind, Irish and I vaulted over the wall. We sprinted to the sidewalk along the canal, falling further behind with every step. A couple stood on the deck of their boat, watching the TBOs race away with our Dixon. We didn't ask permission to board.

"Take care of them," I shouted. "I'm driving."

"You take care of them. I'm the better driver."

"The hell you are." Still, I untied us from the pier. "Get off," I ordered, leaping back onto the boat.

"We are not leaving." The stubborn voice was distinctly Scottish. "This is our—"

Irish opened it up, flying away from the pier, going Fast and Furious on the maritime laws. "I could arrest you for interference with a police action. If you're smart, you'll stay seated. If I tell you to get down, do it."

"That's blood on his arm," the woman said to her husband. Then she looked at me. "Take us back. You can have the boat." The man sat stoically in complete disagreement with his wife.

"There's a seventeen-year-old kid on that boat and he's hurt. Do as you're told and we'll bring you back as soon as we can." I went to Irish, holding onto the frame of the windshield as we skipped over the water. Irish picked his path among the waves and wake. The engines roared, overpowering voices. As fast as we raced, the air was frigid, the sun doing nothing to warm me.

The boat we chased wasn't made for speed. Empty fixtures were mounted to hold fishing poles. Where the driver stepped up to the helm, an adjacent doorway went below where likely a kitchenette and nap/shagging lounge awaited. The boat was built for pleasure.

Ours was built for business.

With every moment, we closed the gap. One man drove, his head on a swivel between us and the water ahead of him. Dixon sat or knelt, but he was looking at us. His hair whipped in the wind. The third man had one arm wrapped around a post, steadying himself as he aimed at us.

Irish cut left, then right. There was nothing smooth about the slalom as we crossed the fishing boat's wake.

"Get down," I ordered our collateral damage. "Get low and stay low." I didn't look to see if they compiled. Their funeral. TBO3 fired, the sound like little New Year's Day poppers. I pulled a gun from Irish's holster. I aimed but couldn't fire. Not with Dixon where he was. "Damn it."

I lost Dixon, his head dropping below the side. Then a long leg snapped out. Dixon kicked TBO3 in the gun hand. The weapon flew up and out of the boat. TBO3 punched down, then kicked. I fucking went Vesuvius knowing Dixon was on the receiving end. Any rational thought I had was replaced with the single goal of tearing the fucker limb from limb. "Get us next to them. I'm going over."

"Next to him? That only works in movies," Irish yelled. "This is not a movie."

"I'll get you there." The owner stood behind us, steady despite the speed and movement. "Step aside, lad." With the Master at the helm, the temperature dropped another five degrees as we picked up speed. There was more air beneath us than water as we freaking flew across the lake. The Master herded the fishing boat, pushing it closer and closer to the coastline, effectively locking down its maneuverability. "Take cover!"

Bullets zipped by like wasps, stinging the fiberglass behind us.

"What's your plan?" Irish pulled a knife from his boot, then handed it to me.

"See what you can do about the driver. I'll handle TBO3 and we'll bring him back for a nice little chat. If we can't get the TBOs under control quickly, we'll jump overboard and leave it to you to cover our asses."

He gripped the back of my neck. "Live to fight another day."

"You know it."

"You ready, lass?" Master at the Helm shouted over the power of wind and machine. "I'm going to approach at an angle. Your window is gonna be tiny. You miss it, we'll back off and try again. Hold tight to something as we approach. It's going to be rough."

"Yes, sir." I braced off Irish, climbing onto the bench. The distance between here and there wouldn't be much. Three feet. Five feet. On land, it would be a hop, skip, or a jump. Vehicle to vehicle, both moving up and down as well as side to side, this would be a long jump, without the run up.

"Ten...nine...eight..." the Master counted, inching closer.

I picked my landing spot, the white center of the suddenly too-small deck.

"Seven...six...five..."

TBO3 fought with Dix, the latter not cooperating.

"Four...three...two...GO!"

My body acted before my head reacted. I saw TBO3's eyes

widen as I cleared the side of the fishing boat. I touched down—feet, knees, hip, shoulder. TBO3 came at me with fists. His bark was bigger than his bite, as the wet floor and evasive maneuvers put and kept both of us on our asses.

Master pulled away and our ride smoothed out. TBO3 wanted to use his fists again. I rolled, using my legs to sweep his out from under him. He lost one leg but kept the other. Then his hand was in my hair, pulling my head back. "I am sick of seeing your face."

I drove back, my head into his. "Same here, pal." My elbow into his gut. My heel into his knee. The restraint on my head was gone. I brought my leg around in a roundhouse kick, hoping to knock him into the driver.

Instead, he tumbled through the open door to the deck below.

I looked around, finally having a sliver of time to assess the situation. TBO5 was still driving. He and our Master were playing a game of hydro bump-and-run. The situation was too fluid, the motion too dynamic. Irish couldn't get a shot.

I could live without a suspect to interrogate. I couldn't live without Dixon.

"How you doing, Dix?" I lifted his hand from his hip, afraid of the damage I'd find. His b-ball shorts had a long, thin cut. Beneath he was a bloody mess. There was a major artery in that general vicinity. If it had been cut, we were on borrowed time. I looked into his face, young and afraid, and lied my ass off. "Just a scratch."

He looked to a waiting Irish. "I don't think I like boats."

"You were on a boat this morning and liked it fine. On your feet now. Take this." I shoved the life preserver into his hands and guided him toward the side of the boat. "Keep your head up. Irish is coming for you." The Master had looped around away, positioning for the pick up.

"What about you?" Dixon let go of his hip to fish one arm through the foam circle.

"I'll be right behind you." He jumped as I shoved to get him as far away from the engines as I could. Then it was my turn—I was yanked backwards. My breath was gone. The deck under my back stole it. My head felt split in two, sound dull and deafening at the same time. A new face floated above mine, distorted and out of focus. It grinned.

And I realized the problem.

I'd miscalculated. There were three TBOs on board, not two.

Sunlight flashed off metal. Pain exploded, a bright flash rivaling the sun.

Darkness took me.

"Nine shine dine fine." The coarse, guttural rhyme penetrated the depths of nothingness to the place where I laid. Dark. Silent. Numb. The sounds I didn't ask to hear were a hand to my collar, dragging me through the innumerable fathoms to the surface.

Intellect came an instant before awareness. I noted my breath and kept it the same. With the dam of unconsciousness breached, information poured in.

Pain led the charge. My head had a heartbeat all its own. Each pulse was a gong strike to my noggin. My neck hurt with the weight of my head pulling on it. My shoulders ached, my arms stretched behind me.

Gone was the boat, the lake air, the motion of the waves. I was on solid ground. I hadn't been here long. My clothes were still wet. I shivered involuntarily in the chilled Highland temperature.

Next came the realization: I wasn't alone. Three voices—two male, one female—were having a hell of a row. In German.

Damn, if I survived this, I was renewing my Babble subscription and learning to *Deutsch sprechen*. I'd skip the lessons on ordering in a restaurant, going straight to hostage negotiation techniques.

A familiar scent permeated my train of thought. Having traveled through dozens of countries, hundreds of cities, I can tell you people are the same. Color. Ethnicity. Religion. Ideology.

None of it matters.

How do I know?

Because the stank of stale human piss is the same everywhere.

Oh sure, it may take longer to get to the stank stage in the polar regions, but once it's there, there's no going back. Not without a gallon of bleach.

The argument went up an octave. In the growl-ravaged rant, I heard my name.

One of the voices grew closer. I willed my muscles to be slacked, to keep up the façade of unconsciousness.

A hand fisted in my hair, my head yanked back. Another hand slapped my right cheek. This sting meant to wake, not hurt.

Cue groan. Fade to giggle. "I told you, Pepe, I'm not that kind of girl."

Pause. "*Wer ist Pepe?*"

Indistinct sounds of general confusion.

"Diamond." My name was enunciated, punctuated with another rap on my cheek. "Wake."

I played the role expected. I inhaled deeply, like you do in the morning when you wake on your own. My lids fluttered, partially planned, partially to control the painful influx of light. I opened my eyes to the first sight of my environment: a sagging plaster ceiling stained yellow, brown, and browner.

The hand in my hair released me, allowing me to lift my head. It was TBO3, the last of the originals. Last time I saw him, he was swan diving to the fish boat's lower deck. Guess it was too much to hope he broke his neck. "Welcome, Diamond. We have been waiting to talk with you."

I smiled as though seeing a long-lost friend. "It's nice to be back. I have to say, you could have done better on the accommodations." The walls were urine-yellow with dirty white showing along the cracks. Dents dotted the inside wall, the shape and size of human heads. The floors were wood, stained with the blood, sweat, and piss of many. "Have you tried Febreze?"

TBO3 curled his upper lip. "*Ja.* You should have smelled it before. But, as you Americans say, beggars cannot be pickers."

"Choosers. Not all choosers are pickers, but all pickers are choosers."

"Enough." The man giving the order was of average build, his hair short and thick, the color of straw. He paced like a fighter, light on his feet. He was their ace in the hole, so to speak, the man in the bow of the boat. "This is the one?"

"Yes, Leo. She is the one from Edinburgh." TBO3 stiffened, snapping to attention. Gone was all the "friendly" in the banter. He was afraid of this man. Leo Krause. This was the second in command of the DPB and, from the reaction of TBO3, the enforcer.

"She knows the formula." The voice was female and desperate.

I twisted to look over my shoulder, straining my aching head to see the voice. There sat the blonde on the top of my mostly-likely-to-kill list. Hanna Lang. Looked like I wasn't the only one who miscalculated. This situation, undefined as it was, required finesse. "What's a bitch like you doing in a nice place like this?"

Hanna Lang strained against the ties holding her to a chair. "I hate you."

"Right back at you, sister." I rolled my eyes, then greeted the thug-in-charge. "Leo Krause. I wondered when we would meet. What are we doing here?"

Leo planted his hands on the arms of my chair, lowering down until we were eye to eye. "What we are doing here is ensuring the integrity of the German nation. What you are doing here," he paused for dramatic effect, "that is to be determined. I am done playing your games. This is my world. If you are useful to me, we will have a long, long time together. If you are not..." He tipped my chair back, my feet dangling in the air. "If you are not, our time together will be short and painful, I promise."

Looking in Leo's eyes, I saw what he was. Someone who flouted laws. Someone who lied to everyone around him. Impulsive. Aggressive. Remorseless. Psychologists had a name for him.

Psychopath.

Agency-approved psych courses taught me how to dig into what made badasses like Leo tick to work a situation to my benefit. I wasn't in a position for a shrink session, and a wrong move could make him explosive. That's the way I read TBO3's expression.

I did have a few things going for me.

One: My hands, and only my hands, were taped together. They were bound behind the chair. Not through. Two: My phone was on the table behind Karl, lit up with a text coming through. If my phone was live, so was the signal leading Irish and friends to me. Three: I had Raven. Hello? Leverage.

"I can see you are not so convinced of what I say." He let the chair go. The legs struck the floor with a thud, jarring my head.

His wick was definitely short if my moment of inner dialog insulted him. "You haven't said anything Leo, not yet. What is it you want from me?"

Leo's face turned nasty. "Blood." He pulled a six-inch knife from a sheath on his hip. Eyes on me, he barked at TBO3. Hands came behind me, tore open the top of my shirt, then pinned my shoulders back. Leo changed his grip on the knife and was on me. I kicked, snapping my leg with the intent to break his arm. He knocked my leg aside and then straddled me, pinning me in place. The blade carved through skin into muscle over my heart. I breathed through it, refusing to scream, determined not to give this fucker anything.

I was ready to die, but not here, not this way.

When I left this world, it would be on my terms.

I'LL TAKE MY ODDS OVER EASY WITH A SIDE OF BACON

A phone rang. TBO3 released me. He answered, spoke. I followed enough to understand Karl was on the other end. Leo shoved my head, an insult, a show of how little he thought of me. Behind me, the voices of the two men alternated until, with a click of a door latch, all was quiet.

My chest burned where Leo carved a diamond over my heart. The crimson lines seeped, wept down my shirt. It wasn't going to kill me but was the reason I'd kill him.

But first things first.

I scooted and hopped until I faced Hanna Becker Lang. "What the hell are you doing here?"

"Negotiating for Damon's freedom. Once and for all." She was harassed, her hair a mess, her voice worn as if she'd spent three hours at a rock concert.

I waited for the real answer to replace the sarcasm. Didn't come. I laughed in her face.

"Stop it. Stop laughing at me."

"So much for brotherly love, huh?"

"My brother doesn't know I'm here. Once he does, Leo will be strung up by his toes and Linus will be fish bait." She tossed her hair, like a princess...or Miss Piggy.

TBO3's name was Linus? He'd pissed me off enough to go

from disposable goon to bad guy I intended to harm in a most irreparable manner. I guess he earned a name.

"You thought, what? You would walk into your brother's secret hideout, proclaim your love for Damon to Leo and Linus, and walk out with a get-out-of-jail-free card?"

"Love? Ha! Leo doesn't understand love. He understands one thing. Money. Power."

"That's two things," I said, because it was. But I heard what she was saying. It went with the psychopath profile. Leo was about power, his power. Rational arguments would hold no weight unless they fed his perception of his authority and status.

Hanna shrugged, details beneath her. "Karl wants a weapon. Leo wants the credit for giving it to him. I want out. Everyone is satisfied."

I bluffed like I've never bluffed before. "You don't have Raven. Neither does Damon."

A wicked, conniving grin spread across her face. "But you do."

I played innocent. "What we had was destroyed. You know that."

She shook her head. "You drugged us. You worked alone for five hours. There was more."

"You're awful sure of yourself."

"Of course, you deny it. I expect nothing else. But it doesn't matter. What will set Damon free is in your head."

I snorted. "You really think I'll give Raven to your brother? You saw what it did. Did your moral code crumble when you realized the terrorist behind all this was your brother?"

"My brother didn't kidnap Damon. Your government did."

"My government didn't toss Damon's office or carve a threat into your dining room table." With a silent click, another puzzle piece fell into place. "You did that. You hired the fortune hunters, too. The Cleaning Ladies and others. You had to beat your brother's teams to the formula."

"I had to find the Raven before Leo. You see how he is. With it, I could remove the death threat to Damon and the other two scientists. Everything could have gone back to normal."

Her logic had more holes than Swiss cheese. "You are fucking delusional if you think there was ever a chance for normal. Four governments who can't agree on how to say the word 'tomato' think your brother and his crew are terrorists. They aren't going to let you go back to normal. If your brother isn't already on the run, he soon will be. He's not going to let you go back to normal. And, just to be clear, there is zero chance of me giving up Raven. I'd die before it falls into his hands."

A thin, knowing smile graced her lips. "That's what I'm counting on."

Her face revealed the answer to the question I hadn't had time to ask. "You told them where we were." My voice was quiet; she'd stolen my breath.

"Once Karl has you, he doesn't need Damon. You proved you have it. Thank you for that. Leo wasn't believing me until you posted the video." She cocked her head. "You're too skinny for a bikini. Better stick to something that covers more. Oh, wait. It doesn't matter. You'll never see another beach party."

I tipped my chair over sideways.

"What are you doing?"

Using my legs, I wiggled the chair down until my arms slid over the top. Then I was on my feet. The folding table against the wall was messily covered with my personal property, electrical tape, scissors, and Hanna's shit.

"You can't cut the tape. They used half the roll."

I knelt and pinned Irish's knife between my boots. Knees spread wide, I could see enough to avoid adding my own scar. The tape was thick, yes, but it was taut. The sharp blade did what it was crafted to do.

"You can't do that. You *can't* do that." She gasped as I stood. "Leo! Linus!"

Swiftly, I peeled the tape from my wrists and covered her mouth. "Now, now. Big girls fight their own battles."

"Uhtymeh."

"Untie you? I don't think so." I stalked behind her, pulling her hair away from her face.

Hanna thrashed left and right, freaked out she couldn't see me, afraid because I was touching her.

"I've been working my ass off to get to the root of the matter and get Damon out. Do you know how much faster I could have gone," I leaned close, whispering in her ear, "if you told me Karl was your fucking brother?" I wanted to scream, rant, rage, but bad guys could walk back any minute and I wasn't ready. So, I whispered. Sometimes, quiet is so much louder than a scream.

Hanna shook her head, denying the facts.

"You knew from the start Karl didn't have Damon. You knew Karl wanted him and the remaining scientists. Two were dead. You didn't care who else died, as long as it wasn't Damon."

She shook her head emphatically.

"It's just us girls, Hanna. No need to lie. Especially when I know I'm right. You see, you didn't just give me up to Leo...you gave up Irish and Popov...and Dixon."

The head that had been on a swivel, froze.

"That's right. Linus and his friends didn't find me, they found Dix. He was going to the grocery store. He'd eaten all the cereal, well, and everything else. By the time I got to him, Linus had him pinned to a wall, using him as a punching bag."

She shook her head again, a different kind of denial.

"He sliced his hip, then used him as a shield to get to their boat."

She mumbled a question. The one I was afraid to ask. Was Dix alive?

"I don't know. And so, you'll understand, I'm really pissed at you." I was behind her again, combing her hair into a thick tail.

Hanna twisted, turned. She tried to escape. She tried to beg.

"You, being a psychologist, specializing in childhood trauma, understand what that kind of experience can do to a teen. Assuming he's alive." I sectioned her hair, taking a firm grip on the front left section. The blade wasn't efficient on the individual strands, pulling hard before cutting.

Hanna screamed, fought, bucked. A patch on the back of her head came with roots. I was balancing out the right side when she butted into the blade, highlighting a section in shades of pink.

I stepped away from her and the hair that had fallen around the chair. "Pray Dixon's alive. Pray to whatever god will claim you." Returning to the table, I took the gun left behind. Checking if it was loaded, I wondered if it was Hanna's. The Sig Sauer P238 matched her style. No matter, it was mine now. My phone flashed to life with a quick swipe of a code, proving a good case was worth the money. A dozen notifications popped up including one warning me I had ten percent charge left. I opened a text to Irish.

Each word counted. *Am fine Dix ok?*

Talky bubble. Talky bubble.

Yes. I am too. Thanks for asking. Coming for you. Then I'm going to kill you.

I smiled. Classic Irish. I prowled to the front windows. Three floors below was the hard reality of a narrow road. No fire escape or other means of egress. The only way out was the front door.

That same door opened. Two had gone out, five came in. These odds sucked.

The man in the middle cleared the doorway and began swearing. When I sound like that, I'm swearing, but as it was in German again, I may be making an ass out of you and me. He crossed the room quickly, going to one knee next to Hanna. He peeled the tape from Hanna's mouth. His manner was gentle, his tone aggressive. Leo's name was prominent in the rant. Allow me to interpret by inference. "What the fuck, Leo? You're an asshole for tying up my sister and cutting off all her goldilocks." One of the men handed him scissors, and Hanna was free.

"Hanna's a bitch," Leo said, emphatically pointing to said bitch. "Tying her up was the only way to stop her traitorous ways."

Hanna surged to her feet, rubbing her wrists. "You are a toad, Leo, a first-class douche bag and cut-rate mastermind. Karl, you could find a better number two recruiting from the International Association of Passivists."

Leo stepped in front of Karl. He and Hanna were going at it, shouting so fast I couldn't keep up the translation. They were pointing, wildly gesticulating, doing everything short of touching each other.

Karl looked like he had a migraine. He was trapped between the two, metaphorically speaking, hand to the bridge of his nose. Under six foot, Karl was solidly built, especially around the beltline. For a man who built his reputation blowing up soft targets, he didn't have a big stage presence. He looked like a banker, a businessman.

Him I could work with.

"English!" The noise stopped as though a switch had been pressed. "As entertaining as this is, it's losing something in translation." I trained the gun on one of the packages of fresh meat. The one on the left looked like he had a hair-trigger. "Keep them holstered."

Karl glanced to the men standing around him. With a small wave of his hand, they subsided. "I am Karl Becker. You are?"

"Diamond. It's about time you showed up. I was beginning to wonder if we were going to wrap up this party without meeting the guest of honor. I have a thing or two to say about how you treat a business partner." Karl's DPB was exactly the kind of organization I had spent my CIA career dismantling. I had skills here once. I hoped they hadn't gotten rusty.

"You have this serum? I understood the formula was lost." Karl skimmed over Hanna, challenging the story she'd told.

"The formula was buried more than lost. I found it. I produced it. You saw the video." I had to assume Karl knew everything Hanna did, which limited my lies. "The professor can't make it. He never could. Knoll Klemer and Monica Hass were the brains behind the science. I hear they aren't available."

Hanna's eyes were going to pull a muscle the way they were whipping between me and Karl. She was thinking through her plays, same as me. She wanted Damon away from Karl and away from me. Her challenge was she had nothing to barter with.

Then she spoke up. "She is right, Karl. Damon Marten is incapable of reproducing the protocol. He has been working on it for weeks and not produced a useable sample. He was a waste of our time. The Brits did us a favor taking him; they brought us her. Diamond. She made the serum once before."

Twice, but who's counting?

She rubbed her brother's shoulder. "Take her to your compound, she can make you as much as you want. You keep your ten million."

The bitch! She was betting with my money.

The nerve of some people.

I opened negotiations with flattery. If you're going to set the table, there's no harm using the good china. "I've done my research, Karl. The DPB has matured under your leadership. Your father had the idea but not the vision to take a local group national. You have the stamina to be in it for the long haul and the tenacity to see it through."

What did I want out of our summit? First, Dixon back in the States and eating Taco Taco Taco until it came out of his ears. Second, Damon permanently extracted from the world of weapons of mass destruction. It was the job I was hired to do. It was the job I would complete.

Me walking out of here alive. Let's not forget that detail.

There was a twist on an already delicate deal. Hanna was a double agent, pretending to be on my side when she was really on her own. Actually, she was a triple agent, because her brother thought she was on his side, too. No. Hanna was on whatever side got her and Damon to a four-bedroom house in the suburbs with two-point-five kids and a dog named Mike.

I didn't give a damn about Hanna except to the extent she

could sabotage me. Oh wait, she nearly got Dix and Irish killed. Things weren't going to end well for her. I began a slow circle of the room, with every step coming closer to the only door.

"My father thought the stage was the most effective way to change minds. I do not." The entourage closed around him as I neared. Karl stilled them with a single hand movement, allowing me to approach.

"I don't care about politics. This is a business; you are a buyer. I can walk away from here without a second thought." One of his men snorted in challenge. I ignored him. "But I'm not going to do that. I like that you're here. Face-to-face is a must these days. I like your money, although it's true, I like everybody's money. And, I like your purpose. Just like Germany, the U.S. is being overrun by outsiders. I don't have anything against them. I just want them to stay where they are." Living in Washington, D.C., I had a plethora of street-corner, demonstration-leading, social-media-flooding rhetoric to pull from. I tweaked and adjusted until his eyes flashed, the silent equivalent of having a fish on the line. I started reeling.

"Exactly." Karl stepped toward me, his sharp eyes measuring my sincerity. "What is the saying? You do not have to go home, but do not stay here. We are alike, yes?"

No. "Enough that I will still sell Raven. Even after this stupid stunt. But there does need to be compensation. I want to be your supplier, your sole supplier."

"Good. The price agreed to was ten million." He held out his hand.

"For the serum, yes." I waved my hand to indicate the slum we stood in. "An additional two for Leo's poor manners." I pulled my shirt away, revealing my personal blood diamond.

"Fuck, Leo." That was the last I understood of the tongue-lashing Karl delivered as he backed Leo across the room. Leo tried explaining, but each time he opened his mouth, Karl slapped it closed. By the time Leo shut up, his lip was split, and his cheek cut.

Note to self, Karl wore a thick ring.

Karl came back to me, wiping his mouth with the back of his hand. "Ten for the serum. You killed several of my men. That," he waved his fingers at my chest, "that is hardly more than an inconvenience. Any payment would be lost in the decimals."

He didn't have money, not the way the TBOs thought. He was running his own bluff. "I want the scientist."

"No." Hanna stepped between us. "They know each other. She's pissed at me and is trying to use him to get even."

I shrugged. "She's right, Karl, I am pissed at her. I'd rather have her but, since she's your sister, I don't expect you'll hand her over. But the scientist is different. She has him. I want him."

Karl looked down at Hanna. "How would taking the scientist get even with you?"

Hanna paled, sputtered like a motor out of gas. "She...she's trying to undermine me with you. She wants me to look like I failed you."

There was another revelation. Karl didn't know Hanna was nailing her target. And Karl, being the ultra-white nut he was, would not like his sister being the white bread under Damon's Nutella.

"I never expected you to succeed in getting the formula. You were the distraction I needed. Papa was right, the only useful part of a woman is between her legs."

Revelation correction. Karl expected Hanna to bed Damon. He had no idea she had fallen for the professor.

"Talk like that, Karl, will have the price going up. I don't really care if you're a misogynistic asshole as long as you remember whose ass you're kissing." I stood in front of the door now. Freedom was five short feet behind me. "When will you have the money?"

"One day, maybe two."

"Wire the money and I'll text you with the drop."

He shook his head, but I didn't expect him to be *that* gullible. "We will exchange money and product at the same time."

“Electronic deposit, Karl. I’m not driving across Scotland with that kind of cash. And I want the scientist.” I stared pointedly at Hanna. “And I want my bags back.” When I refocused on Karl, I was the consummate professional. “Let me know when funds and merchandise are available, and we’ll put this experience behind us.”

And I walked out the door to a battered landing.

I expected them to stop me and was ready to fight. I was grateful words were the only weapons I used. I wasn’t in the mood for another fight. There wasn’t a place on my body that didn’t ache. Time to exit before someone changed their mind. My flight wasn’t fleet. My balance was off, my head pounded. I pushed open the door and stepped out into a shaded street. The tall buildings along the narrow street protected my eyes from the naked sun. It was dinnertime, meaning this entire episode had taken less than two hours.

I couldn’t be that far from Fort Augustus. Since DPB’s budget ran more to stolen cars than airplanes, I guessed I was somewhere near Loch Ness. Irish was coming for me, but I couldn’t hang around here for my ride. My phone was down to eight percent charge. I opened a mapping app. Scotland appeared, the entire country.

Oh and, fun detail, my vision was blurred again. Fucker concussed me.

The you-are-here circle throbbed, throbbed, froze. The screen went black.

Okay, people found their way long before mapping apps. Time to go old school. Out on the street, I didn’t find a “you are here” sign. Or, in my case, a yyoouu aarree hheerree sign. The buildings tucked up against each other, the trucks too big for the road, I could have been on any industrial street in any old town. I arbitrarily went left, needing to put some distance between me and Karl’s crazy crew. I turned a corner. The narrow street began to climb, the added effort exhausting. I needed a defensible place to wait. Up ahead, the road widened at a larger intersection.

Beyond, a structure rose as a beacon.

Inverness Castle.

Having my bearings, I headed for Kevin's pub. The walk wasn't scenic. I wasn't in the sexy part of Inverness. With each step, the pounding in my headache went up a notch. Now that I wasn't under threat of death, I felt the sledgehammer wailing away. The bright day hurt my eyes without the shadows protecting me. The old sign hanging from rusty hinges was my oasis in an urban desert.

"What the holy fuck happened to you?" Kevin came out from behind the bar. "You're a bloody mess."

I gave him my winning smile. "You always had a way with words. I may be sick. Soon."

Kevin had a room he kept for favorite customers needing an alternate place to sleep for a night. It was small, not much bigger than a closet with a single bed, a table from his pub, and two chairs. The overhead light was off but still my eyes were closed. Kevin hummed as he tended my head, working by the small desk lamp he'd brought in.

The door opened and Irish walked in. I knew him by scent, by instinct.

"Thanks for the call, Kevin. How bad is she?"

"Oh, 'bout half as bad as you were the last time I patched you." There was superiority in his tone. "She has a concussion. Someone walloped on her. Twice. Then there's this."

My shirt collar was pulled back, then I felt breath on my face. I opened my eyes to Irish's dark browns staring into mine. How a man could be deadly and pretty at the same time was a mystery to me. "Thanks for coming."

"Your pupils are dilated." His hand went to my cheek, studying my eyes.

"Your nose is crooked." My hand went to the knot on the bridge of his nose.

He smiled, just enough. "That's your fault."

"I wanted to give you something to remember me by." Our

first meeting. I'll have to tell you the story sometime. "Dixon is good? What about your arm?"

"Our Dixon is a survivor. The knife skimmed his hip bone, missed the artery. Popov fixed him up, taught him how to sew his own wound. He's sore but jumped onto the new computers that arrived. I don't know what he was doing, but I don't want him coming after me. He was looking every inch of a Dullahan. Give me a dark alley any time."

"Dullahan?"

"An Irish death-omen on horseback who carries his grinning head and cracks a wicked whip. He says your name, and"—he snapped his fingers—"you're dead."

"Of course. The name had slipped my mind." I ran a light hand down his arm. There was a bandage under his shirt. "And you?"

"Through and through. Missed the bone. Popov sewed me up, too. Dixon wanted to practice his hand on me." He shook his head, chuckling at a memory he didn't share. "What happened on your end?"

I caught him up. "Funny how I barely noticed my head when I was in that room. Now, I just want to crawl into a dark hole for a few days, sleep it off."

He lifted my shirt to study my souvenir. It had to look ugly. Kevin cleaned it with Listerine. Or maybe it was bleach. "What be the name of the dead man who gave you this?"

"Leo. But he's mine," I said, reading his face.

He let my shirt fall closed. "Finders keepers. We have two days to plan for the exchange? How do you see it ending?"

I gave him the smile that shook a mountain.

DEFENESTRATION? THAT WAS SO LAST CENTURY.

Today would be long, but these days often are. After all the time and energy invested into preparation, there was an anxiousness to get on with it already. Those who cave and rush in are usually those carried out. So, we took our time. Irish and I arrived at our destination just after midday. Scotland's Castle Urquhart. First, how you say it. Listening to the locals, it is pronounced *er-kit*. Say it fast and sharp. Second, what is it. A ruin of a medieval fortress. The castle was blown up in the fifteen hundreds by troops garrisoned here rather than turned over. That means you cannot blame me for any of the damage you see today. Third, why here. This was a very cool place, perfect for my kind of mayhem, and exactly where you'd expect to find a diamond.

We wore hats and sunglasses with light jackets, appropriate for the fifty-degree temperature. Fahrenheit, of course. Three days after the Loch Ness affair, my head had gone from bass drum to snare drum. My eyes were the worst, not able to take the bright sunlight. Darkly shaded lenses brought the pain down to manageable. Damn concussion.

Our stage for the exchange was the castle's tower. There were several viable options on the grounds, but the tower called to me. It was square, rising only a few floors, with a narrow staircase—easy to control. The room on the third floor was open and uncluttered. It could comfortably hold thirty or so people. The space was private, and it was cool as ice. Three times we climbed the tower. The first time, we planted the cameras masquerading as rocks, giving us eyes on every angle inside and outside the building.

The second time, we planted weapons Popov handed to us at the water's edge. He and Trixie were out on Loch Ness, masquerading as boaters. They were our backup and our escape route. I had expected Trixie to return Stateside, but the night with Popov had extended her travel plans. Her skills were a nice addition to the team.

The third time entering the tower was a dry run. Popov and Trixie were in our ears, calling off as we passed the checkpoints we'd set.

An hour before the appointed time, Irish and I were leaning against a shortened wall, soaking in the calm expanse of the crazy deep lake and the wild forest behind it. Popov was out there, floating in a high-performance speed boat, rubbing sunscreen into Trixie's barely clad back.

"My turn," he said in our ears.

Trixie giggled, and they switched positions. Popov laid on the padded bench, Trixie straddling him, sitting on his hard ass while she massaged his shoulders. He groaned, deep and low.

"You two are working," I reminded them as their attention was not where we needed it to be.

"This *is* work," Popov blathered. "Hard work."

"I do not want to hear about your hard work, Popov. Sheesh. What happened to professionalism?"

Trixie tossed her hair back. "I am a professional. I earned a certificate in massage therapy when I was undercover in Amsterdam. Physicians write prescriptions for my hands."

"I fucking love Amsterdam. Do my front." Seemingly impossibly, Popov turned over, keeping Trixie in her seat.

"Hey, y'all." That was Dixon's way of saying hello. "A transaction just appeared as pending. There's no dollar amount yet, but the connection was made." Keys fluttered in the background as Dix's fingers flew. Crazy-fast typing, just one of his superpowers. "Put a knife in me you broke-ass, mother-fucking, penniless a-hole." In the three days since, Dix decided he didn't like being beat up, cut up, and taken hostage. His retaliation was about to be unleashed, using weapons like IP addresses, phishing, and bugs.

"Steady, Dix," I said for the nine hundredth time. "We don't want them running off before we get Damon and my bag."

"IknowIknowIknow."

"I have a possible ID." The flirt was gone from Trixie's voice. She was pure Cleaning Lady. "Hanna Lang. She changed her hair, but it's her. She's carrying a backpack."

Popov counted off. "Four are with her. Positive IDs on Damon Marten, Karl Becker, Leo Krause. One other, male."

"Give him a name," I said, turning my back to the lake, casually watching the path from the visitor center down to the castle.

"A name? I gave you three."

"No, for the extra. He's not important enough to get a real name, just something we can use to keep track of him. What do you think of when you think of Germany?"

"Bratwurst." His answer was instant and perfect.

"Bratwurst it is. How do you rate him?"

"Hmm. Maybe seven. He is scanning, ready for trouble, but is out of position. Karl will be dead before Bratwurst can get back to him. Dangerous intent, but needs more training."

"Baby, check out screen two," Trixie said. "More bratwurst."

I glanced at Irish. He grinned, mouthed the word *baby*.

"Two more bratwursts. They are trying to blend in with the tourists. One is in a red shirt with binoculars around his neck."

"Got them," Irish said.

"We should come ashore," Popov said. "More even the odds."

"Stay." Irish's order brokered no argument. "Stick to the plan. No deviations. We are leaving here with the money, the backpack, and the professor. If we can't get to you, we'll take the car."

"Let me come," Dix said, almost whining. "I can help."

"No!" The order was unanimous, in four different accents.

"Don't worry about your Diamond, lad," Irish said, adding his own brand of consolation. "I'm going to take out Bratwurst 2 and 3. Fuck, Diamond, do I really have to call them that?"

"Yes, you do." Despite the very serious situation, I couldn't keep the smile off my face. It was just what we needed to stay loose, limber. "And *we'll* take them out. We still have an hour to go, let's see what they do."

Irish and I moved to a position on a wall farthest from the tower. The wind whipped around us, chilling the warm day. He brought me into the shelter of his body, disguising us as lovers seeking a private moment. I didn't mind his body heat, but my back was to the action.

"I can't see." I tried to trade our positions, but it was like moving an elephant. "Damn it."

"They don't know my face. Stay still."

"Hanna does. I hate being still."

"Don't I know it." His hand moved into my hair, brushing the lump beneath. His face darkened in contradiction to his gentle fingers.

Popov continued the play-by-play. "Karl and his team are staying together. Karl and Leo at the front, Hanna and Damon middle, Bratwurst 1 in the rear. Hanna stepped out of formation. Bratwurst 1 is crowding Damon, now. I'm thinking there's a knife in his back. Hanna is placating, pointing to the visitor's center. Ah, nature is calling. Karl dropped his head and is shaking it."

Irish added color commentary. "A feeling I've had many a time with a female."

I turned my head, punishing the editorial with a bite to his palm.

"Hanna is squeezing knees together. Karl waving her off but

sending Bratwurst with her."

"Where are the other two encased meats? Bratwursts 2 and 3?"

Trixie answered. "Following them across the camera angles. Number 2 is headed toward the cove. And number 3...yes, Diamond, Irish, number 3 is coming your way."

Irish tilted my head up, until his soulful eyes gazed into mine. "'Tis times like these I'm glad you're not a man." He wrapped his arms around me, holding me as he kissed me. It was frustrating, being blind to the enemy behind me, knowing they were close by the way Irish's body hardened. My fingers explored his belt, stopping when I came to a sheath. The snap separated silently. The knife came willingly. I changed my grip, prepared to slash, but Irish settled, the muscles beneath my hand easing.

"Bratwurst 3 is retreating," Trixie called. "Woo, talk about getting a room. Let the woman breathe, Irish."

I slid the knife back onto his hip. "The thing with your tongue, that's new. Trixie, you should get him to teach it to Popov."

"Bah. There is nothing an Irishman can teach me about making woman satisfied. I keep women warm for years with just my little finger."

My phone signaled a text. I slid under Irish's shoulder, reading in the shadow he created. It was Hanna.

We r at the castle. Damon here. K and L and four others. My brother changed. Don't recognize him now. It's my father's fault. We grew up with insanity that killed our mother. It's not his fault.

Irish read the text. "She's switching sides again."

"No, she's always been on the same side. Her own. From the day she suckered you in with a post to the message board, her goal has been to get Damon back. Every time a roadblock was thrown in her path, she adjusted. Over it. Around it. Through it. All that mattered was she kept going. She smiled and played along when we were going her way. She stole from us and betrayed us when she thought she could get a better deal.

Now she believes Karl will not let Damon walk away, which makes us the lesser of two evils."

"You sound like you respect her."

"Not respect, I could kill her for hurting Dixon, but I understand her. If I'd had the opportunity she had, I'm sure I would have done worse."

My brother suspects me. You get D, I'm calling security. K will leave. L will follow. Don't know about the others. 2 guns. All have knives. U owe D. Save him. Get him away from us.

Tell him I love him.

"She's going to get a load of people killed if she calls security. They aren't trained for this level of threat." Irish swore under his breath. "There's a fourth bratwurst. Popov, Trixie, find him."

I read the second part of the text again. Hanna finally accepted what I'd been trying to tell her. You don't just walk away from people like her brother. They keep coming and coming, seeing the enemy everywhere.

"I have three candidates," Trixie said. "The first is by the pigeon aviary."

Irish and I walked at a lover's pace, indulging in the analysis of every male present. We closed on our first target. The man stood at remnants of the many destroyed walls. He studied the grounds and people stretched out below. He lingered in the same spot for too long, refusing to step aside for other visitors. Irish positioned me for a photo, backing up until he collided with the single man in his twenties.

The man stumbled, dropping a notebook. Irish picked it up, fumbling over himself with apologies. He held out his hand to me and we hurried away. "Artist. The pad was filled with sketches of the castle and that woman." He tipped his chin toward a young woman on a lower terrace, wearing the official jacket of the castle staff.

The second man loitered near the entrance, draped lazily in a doorway. His arms were crossed, his gaze scanning the hillside up to the visitor's center. He didn't check his mobile. He didn't pass the time with games. He just watched.

We approached from behind, already being inside the castle. His foot rested on a large stone, pulling his pant leg up to reveal the ankle holster beneath. Irish nudged me before fading into a small room off the main entrance. I counted to ten, then approached the man. Speaking in Russian, I beseeched the stranger to help my husband, who wasn't feeling well.

"*Was hast du gesagt?*" Flummoxed, he forgot his role.

"Husband need doctor. Come now." I switched to English, pulling him, giving him no choice.

"I'm not a doctor," he said in English then.

"Yes, doctor." We entered the room where Irish waited. "Help."

"I said I am not..." He stood eye to eye with Irish. He went for the gun, realizing he was already dead. Irish expertly gripped his head and twisted.

"Bratwurst 4 is down," I said as we quickly searched the body. We stripped him of his weapons and the wire he wore before we positioned him for a nap in the shade.

"Hanna is out of the visitor's center," Trixie announced. "Stay under cover. Karl and friends are entering the castle."

I pulled the baseball hat from my head and put it on Bratwurst 4. Irish and I flattened against the entrance to the room, ready to fight our way out. I heard Karl, recognized his voice as he passed us.

"He was annoyed 4 wasn't in position," Irish said. "Let's see to 2 and 3."

Pulling my hood over my hair, we resumed our happy couple cover and wandered out. We turned into the main walkway, and a short-haired blonde skidded to avoid running into us. Her eyes widened as she recognized Irish. Then her gaze snapped to me. Hanna stepped around us, not looking back as she caught up with her brother. Bratwurst 1 followed her without noticing us.

"She really has to work on her poker face."

"I liked her," Irish said.

"A backstabbing, two-timing manipulator? Says a lot about your taste in women."

He laughed as we drifted toward the water's edge. Our quarry proved elusive. We found Bratwurst 2 but couldn't take action without scarring a family of six for life. Bratwurst 3 led us in a dance. We disengaged as he went back toward the entrance, turning to the small room where we left the former Bratwurst 4.

"Five minutes," Dixon announced. "As soon as they initialize, it's all ours."

That didn't make sense. "Dix, I thought you already had it?"

"Well, I will, you know, as soon as the last lock opens."

I rolled my eyes, hearing my team laughing. "Stay on it until the job is done. Got it?"

"Got it. Does anyone care if I eat the leftover pizza?"

"Order a new one," Popov said. "I'm going to be hungry when I get back."

"People. We are working. Focus." That was Trixie. I know, you thought it was me, but no.

Irish and I casually made our way to the tower. We climbed the stairs, removed the Authorized Personnel Only sign, and continued upward, claiming our position. My hoodie came off—

—"So, is it yes or no to the pizza?"

"You're messing up my inner monologue. Order the damn pizza and shut up."

Where was I? My hoodie came off...I pulled a bulletproof vest over my tank, covered it with a utility vest. The neutered Raven went into one of the pockets. Irish lost his jacket, exchanging it for titanium or whatever they made these vests from currently. He was a one-man arsenal with knives, flash grenades, and guns. The first was his weapon of choice. While Hanna may have wanted undue attention from the guard, we did not.

I double-checked our escape route. The knotted rope hung over the ramparts to a second weapons stash and the docking point for Popov's boat. Ready, I texted Karl using the number for TBO3, wondering with curious affection what became of

Linus. He wasn't part of today's entourage.

"They are on the move. Converging on the entrance." Trixie continued to describe what the cameras caught, even as the footfalls gave the same information.

"Moving into position." I followed Irish down the narrow staircase. He took a knee on the lowest step. I was one above him.

Our field was the room made of stone. Sunlight and wind entered unfettered through the window casings. No glass or screen kept nature from entering. A black bird flew in and landed on a rod that supported modern lighting.

"The rook would move on if it had any sense," Irish said. Then, as if listening, the bird flew out the opposite window. It wasn't a crow, but I took it as a sign. A good one.

"Making the turn at the first landing," Trixie said. "Bratwurst 1 with Damon. Bratwurst 2 with Hanna. Then Karl, Leo, and Bratwurst 3."

"Weapons count." Popov paused. "Knives on Damon and Hanna. Kidneys. Hanna said two guns, but I don't believe. Trixie and I should join in."

"Stick to the plan," I said. "They want Raven, we're going to give them Raven. As long as Karl stays in control, we'll all walk out of this with the same number of holes we came in with. Irish, stay on Leo. He could break."

"I'll be breaking him."

Footfalls could be heard clearly now. The staircase from the lower floor ran along the courtside wall. Irish and I were tucked in the sister staircase on the lakeside wall.

Trixie's voice came into our ears again. "Civilians on the second floor just cleared out. Karl and his crew are starting the climb to you." She had a nice cadence, very Midwestern. She called their movements as smoothly and matter-of-factly as if she called a baseball game.

And the Raging Assholes are taking the field. Stepping out of the dugout is Bratwurst 1, a man whose reputation was worth as much as a three-dollar bill. He's got an arm breaker on Damon Marten. I know they say the pen is mightier than the sword but his Ph.D. isn't looking too good against that knife in his side.

Bratwurst 2 is on the field, manhandling the fair Hanna Lang. A classic switch hitter, Hanna knows her way around the game. No half Nelson for Hanna in this matchup. It's go forged steel or go home.

Next out of the box is the skipper, Karl Becker, followed by his ass-kissing, psychopathic ace Leo Krause. Bring up the rear is the cleanup man, Bratwurst 3.

The Diamond Facets have an all-star lineup. The home team manager is the legendary Diamond, feared and revered by men and women alike. Rumor has it she's lost her edge, so we'll see exactly what kind of game she's brought this afternoon.

Her ace is Sam Irish, a wicked man with a gun for an arm. Three countries claim him, five call dibs on his head.

Yuri Popov and Trixie the Cleaning Lady were picked up off waivers. While his style is brute force and hers is finesse, both of these competitors prefer to be at the top of the lineup. We'll see if these two stick.

Hanna Lang is a lefty infielder who has bounced between sides like a volleyball. Completely unpredictable, it'll be interesting to see how and if Diamond uses this raw talent. If she plays for the Diamond Facets at all.

Our umpire today is "Blind" Damon Marten. Rumor has it, his rule book is written in braille.

Diamond and Karl meet at the plate for the metaphorical handshake. "Nice of you to be on time, Karl, but my bank account is still waiting."

"Don't you trust your partner?"

"We both walk out of here with what we want, then we'll talk about trust."

"As you say."

Neither manager is smiling as they return to their team. It's one hundred percent game face. The Diamond Facets are playing shorthanded today. Looks like someone needs to read the rule book again. Popov and Trixie are deep, deep, deep in centerfield. Diamond is on the mound and Irish is playing well in front of first base. Looks like he's expecting a lot of bunting today. Hanna is behind first, doubling up on the base while leaving second and third wide open. Like I said, she's unpredictable.

At the snap of Karl Becker's fingers, the Raging Assholes take the field. Foregoing the batting quintessential to baseball, Karl employs a defensive offense known as "you can't kill us all." Clearly, he has scouted his opponent.

Bratwurst 1 is playing catcher. He's crowding "Blind" Damon, practically pinning him to the backstop. Personal space, my friend, personal space. Bratwurst 2 is on first base and covering Hanna Lang. Literally. No sunlight sneaking between those bodies. Seems the Raging Assholes need a lesson in social distancing.

The man on second is the second-rate second in command. Look at those fingers twitching. We definitely have an itchy twitchy man in the infield. And in another unorthodox move, the skipper is on third. Bratwurst 3 is right behind his manager, using a deep shift called "shadowman."

Diamond is in the stretch, her eyes going between home plate, the man on third, and the loose cannon on second. Home plate, third base, loose cannon. The runners are tense, looking to steal a base and anything else they can get.

Irish approaches the mound for a conference. His brows are furrowed, creating a trench deep enough to shelter WWI soldiers. Little early in the game for a chat. What's there to talk about? Wedding gifts? "Diamond, stop talking like you're calling a bloody baseball game." And then he turned away. "Bloody nutty woman."

"If I had a million dollars..." The Barenaked Ladies fan-favorite blasted my ear, welcome, even if not in key. The music was interrupted with a hoot, then a holler, and finally a "Got it."

I stared down the man on third, I mean, Karl. "Let's get this done. I have dinner plans." I took a glass vial from my field jacket. “As promised.”

“Hold it there,” Karl said. “Open it. Let Dr. Marten smell it.”

A nice play, totally apropos of a raging asshole. “No. He’s valuable to me. You want a test, use one of your disposable extras.” I was mostly sure this version of Raven wasn’t deadly. I removed the silicone seal.

Karl signaled Bratwurst 3 with a head twitch. Bratwurst 3 hesitated, sensing the trap his eyes couldn’t see. He crept to the center of the room, knife ready to murder me if I tried anything. He sniffed. Then sniffed again.

“I don’t smell anything,” Bratwurst 3 said to Karl, retaking his position.

Karl raised an eyebrow to me. “What game is this?”

“It ain’t baseball.” I rolled my eyes. “Look, the reaction isn’t instant.”

“How long until the effects—”

Bratwurst 3 giggled. He schooled his face. Then giggled again.

Karl studied the man, a delighted, evil grin curled his lips. “Just like on the video. He thinks he’s a bird.” Karl stepped back as Bratwurst 3 unfurled his wings. He flapped them experimentally and then took flight. Leo ducked a wing, Hanna and Bratwurst 2 flattened against the wall behind them. Irish dodged it. Damon stood stock-still, staring, while Bratwurst 1 swatted at the flailing wing.

I glanced at Irish. He nodded imperceptibly. It was time to end this game. I’d make the trade, then get Damon up the stairs to our escape route. Irish would get the pack back and, against my better judgment, Hanna. We had a few surprises along the climbing staircase, in case someone was stupid enough to follow.

The room was focused on the flight of Bratwurst 3. Karl laughed maniacally as Bratwurst 3 passed him again, moving faster now. Leo echoed him.

Irish edged along the wall toward Hanna, freezing when our bird rounded to his side of the room.

Hanna and Bratwurst 2 ducked, so did Irish. Bratwurst 1 did

not, and the full force of a bird-brained bodyguard checked him into the wall. His head bounced off the unyielding stone and he went down, taking the birdman and Damon with him. A human pile of arms and legs was stacked up between a window and my exit route, making my job harder. The heap lurched and Bratwurst 3 launched from the pile, starting another sweeping pass of the room. Irish made his move.

"Ca-caw! Ca-caw!" Bratwurst 3 screeched as he took flight from the top step to the floor below. A very human grunt was immediately followed by another bird call.

Leo squatted on the landing, peering to the lower level. "He is still flying around." He looked to me. "How long will it last?" Leo rose slowly, his jaw clenched.

Bratwurst 2 was a pile of inanimate flesh, and Hanna was Irish's captive.

I was halfway to Damon when Karl put the point of a knife to the professor's throat. "Going somewhere?" he asked.

"Yes," I said, stepping out of his reach, back toward the center of the room. "Time to conclude our business." I held up the vial.

"Annalisa, don't do this." There wasn't fear in Damon's face, there was determination. "I taught you better than this. You will not do it. Do you hear me? You will not!"

Karl pulled his arm back, flipped the knife in his grip, and brought the hilt solidly down on Damon's head. Damon crumpled to his knees, hands to his head, blood pouring out between his fingers.

"NO!" Hanna screamed bloody murder, which was appropriate given the amount of O-positive visible.

Karl pulled Damon's head back, throat exposed. He studied his sister. "What is this I see? Tell me you haven't been stupid enough to fall in love with him." His lips curled in distaste.

She lifted her chin. "I don't love him. This wasn't part of our plan." The tremble in her voice betrayed her. "Get the formula and return home to continue with our father's work."

Karl's lips thinned, the lines in his face deepened. "Of all the people...I never thought you would betray me." His face darkened, hurt turning to hate. He flipped the knife back around, leading with the blade.

"Hey, Karl. Catch." I threw the vial high, toward the window, forcing him to choose between Damon and Raven. Victory surged through me as Karl dropped Damon and the knife. I ran with intent to tackle. A gun fired. One, two, three. No time to register if there was pain. Just two more steps...

A streak of gold, a fragrant breeze, and Karl was gone.

Me and my fucking head bounced off the stone wall. I spun, prepared to take a hit, searching for my target.

Leo laid on his back, two feet behind me, bullet holes in his forehead, throat, and chest. Bratwurst 2 was groaning, slowly coming to. Damon was climbing to his feet, holding on to Irish.

But there was no Karl. Or Hanna for that matter.

Irish pointed behind me.

To the window.

I looked out to the ragged ground between the castle and Loch Ness. Karl Becker's lifeless body was draped across the craggy rock, his unseeing eyes cast to the heavens he would never reach. Hanna lay atop him. Her head on his belly, her arms and legs at unnatural angles.

Sirens approached.

"I was afraid of that," Irish said. "I tried not to use the gun, but that fucker was too close to you. We have to go."

Irish half carried the bloodied and traumatized professor to our escape.

"Five minutes," I said to Trixie and Popov, picking up my backpack. "Three of us."

On the roof, Irish fitted Damon into a harness, attached him to the rope, and put him over the side. Evidence of our presence was gone, taking it all with us as we repelled to the ground. We landed side by side. Two when there should have been three. "Where is Damon? We have to go."

There was only one answer. He'd gone to Hanna. We darted

around the corner. Damon stood stiff as a statue, studying Karl's lifeless form and Hanna atop him. He turned to me, his eyes flooded with tears.

"It's hard to believe it was only a week ago." Dixon marched into my living room, a bag of tortilla chips in his hand. Dixon and I returned home the day after Urquhart. He'd been catching up on American crap food ever since. "I keep expecting to wake up, to find it was all a dream. I mean, we're really millionaires." He lifted his Loch Ness monster T-shirt to show off the hot red line two inches long over his low riding basketball shorts. Over it, the date was written in block letters. Below was written *Loch Ness* in a messy script. "No, it was real. There's the proof. You can look at it any time you need to."

"You need real ink, not marker," Popov said. He and Trixie left Scotland, taking a circuitous route through Amsterdam. They landed on my doorstep late last night and since had occupied the apartment across from MaryAnn McNamara. "On Diamond's next case, you come to Russia. I get you tattoo of a real man."

I snorted. "Number one, Dixon doesn't want a tattoo of a man. Number two, there isn't going to be a next case. One and done. That's my motto."

"Bullshit. I will bet you fifty thousand dollars you have another job within..." He pursed his lips. "One week."

"I will take that bet because it is not gonna happen. Not in a week. Not in a month. Not ever. I don't do for hire." We shook, sealing the sucker's bet.

It was a party, impromptu as it was. This was the first time we were all back together. Popov and Trixie. Irish and Dixon. Damon Marten. Ian Black. It took all of us to put an end to the domestic terrorism of Karl Becker and the DPB.

"You don't need another like this one, too close." Trixie sat curled into Popov, her wine glass nearly empty. "Too close. Next time, we'll be there backing you up. No matter what you say."

"There's not going to be a next time," I reminded her, refilling her glass.

"You take too many risks," Irish said in a tone distinctly different than the others. He leaned against the dining room doorway, looking as though he had somewhere else to be. "You act before you think. Still."

"Hey, I followed the plan." I wasn't whining. "It was Hanna who ran the suicide squeeze play. She didn't wait to see if Karl caught the vial of Raven. She just took him out."

"She did," Irish said. "Right out the window."

Damon left his chair, pacing to work out what he was feeling. "I see it every time I close my eyes. I looked at her when I thought Karl would kill me. I saw it in her eyes."

"What did you see?" Dixon asked.

"Goodbye. She ran straight at me, then she was gone."

Dixon chewed, shrugged. "Death by defenestration. Better than castration, annihilation, and decapitation."

Damon shivered. He drank his vodka and cranberry, soothing feelings too raw, memories too close.

Ian passed a rounded manila envelope to Damon. "I wish I could have been there, but someone had to stick around here and pay the bills. Speaking of bills, I found a house for you in Nova Scotia, Damon. Cash motivated the owner. You can pick up the keys when you get up there. Here are your new documents."

Damon pulled out the small assembly of paper and plastic. "Thomas Smith?"

"The most common name in Canada. You won't have to work, not with the money our boy here got us, but if you do, my cousin has some connections. It isn't a university, but still, a school is a school. Give me your wallet. All the old stuff has to go."

Damon, now Thomas, handed over the standard leather billfold. Ian cleaned out his driver's license, credit cards, AAA card, university ID, and a dozen customer cards. In went the new ID, bank card, even a library card.

Thomas pulled a second driver's license from the envelope. "Aria Smith. We're married?"

"Five years. Congratulations, buddy. Your anniversary is next week. You don't want to forget it."

Thomas nodded, his eyes welling. "I am so sorry I pulled you into this. All of you. I owe you a debt…I can never repay."

I set aside my second-to-last box of Walkers. "Consider us even. I know it will be hard, starting over, but you have the chance at a good life."

"A happy life," Trixie said. "And you'll love Nova Scotia. It's a great place to live and work."

"A quiet life," Damon added hastily. He ran his finger over his wife's license, a soft smile of hope for the future. "I'm not starting with nothing, Diamond. Thanks to you all, I'm starting with everything."

"Wait, I have something for you." I hurried to my bedroom, to the nightside table, in front of Gavriil's picture in shattered glass. Back in the living room, I completed the circle. "Here."

"The Poe anthology. Diamond, I gave this to you."

"And now I'm giving it back."

"Thank you." He clutched it to his chest like a prize. "I have to go. If you ever need an expert in chemistry…call somebody else."

I said goodbye to Damon and to that girl who studied under him. My team offered luck, good wishes, and tortilla crumbs.

"Wait," I shouted before the last hand was shaken. "Do not forget your box."

Damon went to the quiet corner and pulled a sleepy puppy from the cardboard box. "Come on, Lily, let's go bring Mama home."

It was several more rounds of goodbyes, pats on the head (Lily, not Damon), handshakes (Damon, not Lily), and hugs (both). We exchanged promises that would never be kept, then the door closed behind Thomas. The sound was final and brought a lump to my throat. Thomas and Aria Smith had a rough road ahead. Her broken bones were healing, but painful. More surgeries and hours of therapy were needed before she would walk again.

There was always a price to be paid.

Still, they had a future with laughter, and dinners, and arguments ending in love. There would be parties and friends and, maybe, children.

Children. There's a thought.

"Time for us to split, too." Trixie tugged at Popov's hand until he stood. "We have the case that just came in. Remember, Yuri? The one we have to inspect very closely." She enunciated each word, sending him a message they could understand on Mars. She was so pitiful, she was cute.

"Yes. Hands-on inspection," Popov said equally slowly, his ugly face in a broad, hungry grin.

"Pathetic," I said. "Speaking slowly is not an effective code, you two. We all know what you are going to do."

Trixie winked at me as Popov took the lead. "What? A new file just came in I need his expert help on."

Right. Used that one before.

She paused at the door, Popov's hand on her ass. "I was serious about a job, Diamond. A few weeks in the gym, you'll be the woman the enemy loves to hate again."

"Bitch," I shouted, punctuating it with a pillow where her head had been.

And then there were four. Irish, Ian, Dixon, and me. It felt right, having these men close. It felt like home.

"What do you say to a movie and wings?" Ian punched Dixon's arm playfully.

"Yes, yes, yes." Dixon pushed to standing, his body unable to match the enthusiasm in his voice. He was healing. Every day a little better. "Can I drive? Please? I've been practicing. Popov let me drive all over Scotland."

Ian took his keys out, looking at them for an answer. Proving his arms hadn't been injured, Dixon snatched them, then shuffled quickly to the door. "Let's go."

"He's lying, Ian. Popov let him drive once and came back greener than the Scottish Highlands. I don't think he let him in the car after that."

"I figured. He'll get better." Ian shook his head, dropping his voice. "He's got to get better. If you don't hear from me in an hour, send a tow truck."

The door closed. "Guess it's just you and me. Do you want to…" The room was empty. Irish must have slipped out the back. He wasn't big on goodbyes. I don't remember him ever saying the word.

I was alone with empty glasses, empty plates, empty bowls. "A metaphor for my life," I said as I stacked the ceramics and carried them into the kitchen. I washed. I rinsed. I dried and put away. I sought out other jobs, looking across my kitchen. Everything neat.

One chair at my kitchen table. Three crows sat on the windowsill, one looked in. It was nice having company.

It's funny how quickly loneliness can find you, remind you what you all but forgot. Just a moment of quiet, that was all it took.

And there it was. Some people aren't meant to have a happily ever after.

I stalled outside my bathroom. The window screen laid propped in the corner. Glass fragments scattered across the hexagon tiles. Reminders of a job unfinished.

"Did the family go?"

"Fu-uck." I jumped out of my skin. Irish appeared out of nowhere. "Family?" I stalled, buying time to wipe my face, restart my heart. "You mean everyone? Yes, they left. I thought you had, too."

"In due time." He handed me an envelope.

It was sealed with no address, no return. "Nobody says that these days. What's this?"

"It explains itself."

I tore it, careful of the paper within. I opened the tri-fold and found my own handwriting. "Uh, what?"

"Read." He circled behind me, resting his chin on my shoulder.

"'I, the one and only queen of Diamonds, demon tamer extraordinaire'—was I drunk when I wrote this?"

"Keep reading."

"'Demon tamer extraordinaire recognize Sam Irish, and all of his aliases, for his bravery, gallantry, and brainery'—I was drunk. That is not a word, and if it were, it would not apply to you."

"I think you described me to a tee. Keep going. Nevermind, I will." He tore the paper from my hand. "…'bravery, gallantry, and brainery, with three wishes. With the wishes, the queen of Diamonds will do as is asked without arguing, negotiation, and/or/if stalling. This letter is valid until one year after my death.'"

"How many of these things do you have? Is that my signature? I don't think it is. Let me see it. You forged it, didn't you." Which turned into a game of keep-away ending when he fell into me and my single kitchen chair, flattening it to the ground. I laughed, squashed between the deformed metal and Irish's fine chest. "You're heavy," I complained but didn't try to move him. "I take it you want something?"

He nimbly climbed to his feet, extending a gentlemanly hand. "We're going for a ride."

"Where?"

"You promised not to argue, negotiate, or stall. Get your phone, your keys, your womanly things. I'll drive."

I felt like I was in a forest, balancing on one foot, and no matter where I set the other down, it would be into a bear trap. "I need more than that."

He looked away, scratched his head.

"Who's stalling now?"

His glare scalded. Someone didn't like being called out. He

grabbed my wrist, using more strength than he needed, and slapped a small card into my palm.

"'Robin Ransom. Ph.D. HSPP. ABPP.'" When it clicked, it clicked loudly. "Therapy?" The crows outside my window scattered. "No. Not happening. I'm not going to a therapist. And I'm definitely not seeing someone named Robin. You and karma can kiss my ass." I crumpled the card, threw it at him, and went for my bedroom.

He yanked on the wrist he still held, pulling me into him. "A lovely ass it is, but your appointment is in an hour. We best be off."

I shoved him, reiterating what he could do with his therapist. "We best defenestrate you out the kitchen window. I'm not leaving this house. Ever."

Then I was over his shoulder, being run through my own apartment. I grabbed for a door, a lamp, books, bookshelf, anything to stop this stupidity. My curses echoed in the stairwell. Heaven, hell, and everyone in between knew I was pissed.

Su-Chen Wong stood in her doorway, the litter of puppies cheering Irish on. "Bye-bye, now. Bye-bye."

"No bye-bye. Help-help."

"Bye-bye." She waved.

Down a floor, Maryann McNamara leaned against her door frame, sauce on her apron, hand pressed to her heart. "How romantic. You kids have fun."

"Fun?!" I screeched. "Do I look like I'm having fun,"

She closed her door, leaving me to my fate. "It's a conspiracy! Fucking Irish!"

ACKNOWLEDGMENTS

Many thanks to Scotland for being so damn beautiful and inspirational. Fort Augustus, The Highland Club, The Boathouse, The Moorings, the gas station/grocery store, Castle Urquhart, Inverness, and, of course, Loch Ness are real places that I dragged into my fictional world. I adored them all in the short time we visited and highly recommend each and every one. I forgot about the sheep. I should have put sheep in this episode! Ugh!

Diamond asked me to personally thank Chris Rhatigan, editor extraordinaire. She loved what you did with *Suicide Squeeze* so much that she is out looking for new trouble to get into. She wants you to save a spot on your calendar for her. I thank you too.

Thank you to Eric and Lance for standing with Diamond and all your work to bring her to life. Thank you to Kate for dotting the I's and crossing the T's. Thank you to JT for putting your creative talents to work for Diamond's cover. Love the way you get inside my head…and don't run away terrified. You amaze me.

Thank you to those who made this story the best it could be. To my readers Matt, Karen, Traci, and Shannon, honest feedback is the highest form of respect. To Michelle for that final polish. Thank you. To Maria for the medical advice and all of those very graphic links. I might not have been able to read the words, but the pictures told me what I needed. To Aaron for his work on the boat scene and those very graphic links. Who knew bodies could bounce like that? To Jack for plotting and planning with me and for the word "defenestration". To Viktor for figuring out who was on first, and second and third. Without each of you, this story would have been just a little bit…less.

TG WOLFF writes thrillers and mysteries that play within the gray area between good and bad, right and wrong. Cause and effect drive the stories, drawing from 20+ years' experience in Civil Engineering, where "cause" is more often a symptom of a bigger, more challenging problem. Diverse characters mirror the complexities of real life and real people, balanced with a healthy dose of entertainment. TG Wolff holds a Master's Degree in Civil Engineering and is a member of Mystery Writers of America and Sisters in Crime.

On the following pages are a few
more great titles from the
Down & Out Books publishing family.

For a complete list of books and to
sign up for our newsletter,
go to DownAndOutBooks.com.

Moonlight Falls
A Dick Moonlight PI Thriller
Vincent Zandri

Down & Out Books
January 2021
978-1-64396-187-3

If you knew your life could end at any moment, how far would you go to prove you murdered your lover?

Albany, New York, is the dark setting of this paranoid thriller about Richard "Dick" Moonlight, former APD detective turned private investigator, who believes he killed Scarlet Montana—his illicit lover and wife of his ex-boss, Chief of Detectives Jake Montana. Problem is, despite the blood on his hands, Moonlight doesn't remember what happened!

Dark as Night
Mark T. Conard

Down & Out Books
February 2021
978-1-64396-179-8

Morris White is a Sous Chef at a first-rate Philadelphia French restaurant. All he wants is to leave behind his past—the poor neighborhood and petty crime he knew as a kid—and open his own restaurant. His dream comes one step closer to reality when the affair he's having with Vicky Ward heats up. Not only is she the manager of the restaurant, but she comes from money and a privileged background.

The only thing that could stop them from turning their dream into a reality is Morris's half-brother, Vince, who is about to get out of Graterford Prison and is set on exacting revenge against the mobsters who ruined his life.

Ouroboros
Andrew Davie

All Due Respect, an imprint of
Down & Out Books
December 2020
978-1-64396-124-8

McGill and Gropper work as unlicensed PIs who operate out of a diner in Charleston, SC. McGill, the face of the operation, is a former police officer. Now incredibly out of shape, he rarely leaves the diner and has a fondness for pancakes, bacon, and coffee. Gropper is well versed in fighting. He doesn't tend to carry standard weapons as he himself is lethal.

McGill and Gropper take almost any job and are willing to break the rules to get these jobs done. As they conduct business, someone from McGill's past returns to enact revenge.

Deemer's Inlet
Stephen Burdick

Shotgun Honey, an imprint of
Down & Out Books
August 2020
978-1-64396-104-0

Far from the tourist meccas of Ft. Lauderdale and Miami Beach, a chief of police position in the quiet, picturesque town of Deemer's Inlet on the Gulf coast of Florida seemed ideal for Eldon Quick—until the first murder.

The crime and a subsequent killing force Quick to call upon his years of experience as a former homicide detective in Miami. Soon after, two more people are murdered and Quick believes a serial killer is on the loose. As Quick works to uncover the identity and motive of the killer, he must contend with an understaffed police force, small town politics, and curious residents.

CPSIA information can be obtained
at www.ICGtesting.com
Printed in the USA
LVHW030120090221
678694LV00003BA/276

9 781643 961774